Praise for *LEAD beyond Your Title*

"*Lead beyond Your Title* is full of stories and practical tips that will empower you to create amazing experiences for all learners—students, teachers, and administrators. You can't help but be inspired by Nili's passion and authentic experiences as you read this book. Regardless of your position, this message will push you to see how you can leverage your gifts, take the initiative, and make the impact you desire."

—**Katie Martin**, VP of Partnerships at AltSchool,
author of *Learner-Centered Innovation*

"*Lead beyond Your Title* is one part inspiration, one part practical toolbox, and all PIRATE! Nili Bartley shares tons of practical ideas in each chapter. Through her own story, she encourages all of us to be the leader our students and our schools need—not because of our titles but because of the passion and fire within us."

—**Matt Miller**, educator, speaker, blogger,
and author of *Ditch That Textbook*

"If you plan on reading *Lead beyond Your Title,* you better batten down the hatches and prepare for a storm of ingenious ideas to pour your way! Follow Nili Bartley's incredible journey towards becoming an extraordinary PIRATE educator and coach who encourages others to bring their strengths and passions to school every single day. As you read, be sure to pillage all of her creative ideas to use in your classroom or school to build a stronger community and unleash the confidence every child possesses but doesn't always discover! Whether you're a classroom teacher, instructional coach, or administrator, you're holding a treasure trove of ideas for transforming school into a place where every child loves to learn!"

—**Paul Solarz**, fourth-grade teacher, author of *Learn Like a PIRATE*

"An undeniable compilation of wisdom, passion, and vulnerability. Nili shares her own experiences and practical insights on how *you* can lead beyond your title. You are never 'just' a teacher. You *are* a teacher, a leader, and a miracle maker!"

—LaVonna Roth, creator and founder of Ignite Your S.H.I.N.E.®

"Anyone can be a leader. Teacher. Administrator. Student. Parent. Anyone. Titles don't matter. In *Lead beyond Your Title*, Nili lays out the blueprint for becoming a leader from wherever you are. Yes, you will need to venture out. Yes, there will be bumps and bruises. But Nili provides you with inspiration, practical advice, and the motivational tools to bring everyone else along. With this book, you too will be able to find your own leadership path. It doesn't matter where you stand; find your spot and lead from there!"

—Rich Czyz, author of *The Four O'Clock Faculty*

"In *Lead beyond Your Title*, Nili Bartley shows how one inspired person can create change in her students, the staff she works with, and even those who are above her on the organizational chart. Nili shares her 'why' and then gives examples and ideas how teacher leadership can create a culture that helps to make school amazing for our students. With concrete evidence of classroom and schoolwide culture change, Nili shares her passion for what she does and why she does it. For anyone who has ever said, 'I'm just a teacher,' this book will show you how being 'just a teacher' is probably the most important job anyone can have. For school administrators who are looking to support teacher leadership opportunities, here is a recipe for growth that will be hard to match."

—Jay Billy, elementary school principal and author of *Lead With Culture*

"Nili challenges educators to act in the best interest of students, no matter our roles. With messages of 'be true to yourself,' 'include student voice,' and 'be there for others,' she provides hints to help every educator lead with passion within the walls of their own school. Nili helps us identify our beliefs, stay true to them, and then educate others about our *why*."

—**Joy Kirr**, middle school teacher and author of *Shift This!*

"In true 'squeaky wheel gets the oil' fashion, this inspiring leadership manual will serve as grease to lubricate your launch into greatness. Grow alongside edu-hero Nili Bartley as she vulnerably shares her strategies and struggles for firing up her lucky learners and her collegial co-workers in her relentless pursuit to equip and empower. Go all-in as you check out this supercharged must-read, bursting with innovative and intriguing ideas sparked by the purpose and passion of this one PIRATE leader."

—**Barbara Gruener**, author of *What's Under Your Cape?*

"Nili Bartley's *Lead beyond Your Title* is a testament that title or position alone can't make someone a leader. She inspires in her debut compilation of hands-on experiences that reflect her PIRATE commitment and provides leadership strategies that can push us out of our comfort zones into the realm of leadership. What resonates most powerfully in this book is that Nili Bartley is a catalyst and advocate for the possibilities of tomorrow: She is a change agent, an innovation agent, and a passion agent. Nili Bartley embodies the potential superhero in every educator to be a twenty-first-century leader."

—**Brian McCann**, principal of Joseph Case High School, 2018 NASSP Digital Principal of the Year

"Nili Bartley's *Lead beyond Your Title* allows readers to find their inner superhero power to be a catalyst for change. She encourages us to be brave and bold for all learners. Nili shares an honest and fresh perspective of how many educators feel, striving to do innovative work and make global connections in a system that was built in an agrarian era. She reminds us of the importance of transformational and disruptive leadership and that there is beauty in reflection and embracing the power of positivity. We are all change makers, regardless of our titles. Nili suggests to 'pass the mic and let others in' and that we are all pirate leaders, impacting students. We have to start somewhere, even from the ground up. Nili provides authentic resources that can be used immediately in any educational setting from shaking up professional development to building relationships with students and colleagues. She challenges us to chart our own course and go on a treasure hunt to find our inner pirate."

—**Rayna Freeman**, fifth-grade teacher, MassCUE president

"In this passionate and practical book, Nili Bartley provides strategies for building impactful relationships with students, teaching peers, and administration. Her wisdom comes from a rare balance of deep professional conviction and the selfless ability to give voice to the students, teachers, and admin who have influenced her . . . and whom she influences. A heartfelt tale of successful culture change from within, *Lead beyond Your Title* imparts life lessons that go well beyond the domain of education."

—**Andrew Gardner**, VP of Professional Learning, BrainPOP

"When you are raised by a mom who is a Latin teacher, you learn early on that the word education comes from the Latin phrase *e duco*, which means 'to lead forth.' As educators, leadership is truly part of who we are. In her life and now in her book, Nili Bartley exemplifies how leadership and education are intertwined. Her passion is visible in her actions, and in her book, her passion practically jumps off every page. It does not matter what your title is; what matters is if you are sharing your passion more than following your job description. In true PIRATE fashion, this book packs a double whammy of awesomeness: inspiration to get every educator fired up for kids *and* specific ideas and examples to nudge (or shove) you out of the traditional education toolbox. Whether you are charged with a district of thousands or whether you are guiding the learning of a small group, you are an educator, you are a leader, and you need to read *Lead beyond Your Title*."

—**Liz Garden**, principal of Dr. Leroy E. Mayo Elementary School, co-founder of MomsAsPrincipals

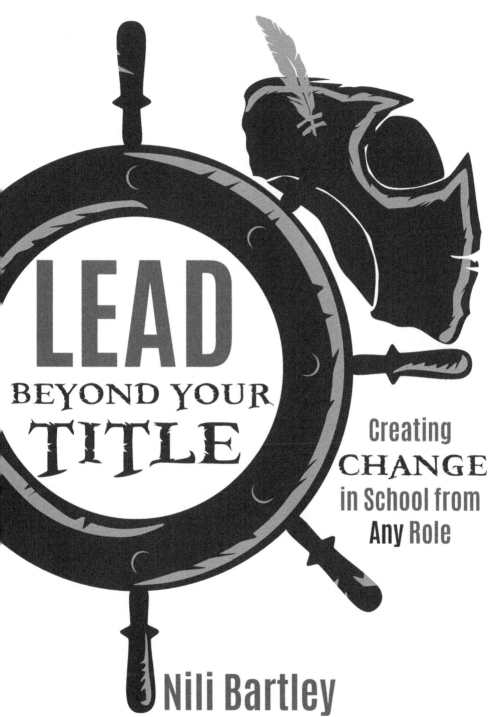

A **LEAD** Like a **PIRATE** Guide

LEAD
BEYOND YOUR
TITLE

Creating CHANGE in School from Any Role

Nili Bartley

Lead beyond Your Title
© 2019 by Nili Bartley

This book is available at special discounts when purchased in quantity for use as premiums, promotions, fundraisers, or for educational use. For inquiries and details, contact the publisher at books@daveburgessconsulting.com.

Published by Dave Burgess Consulting, Inc.
San Diego, CA
DaveBurgessConsulting.com

Cover Design by Genesis Kohler
Editing and Interior Design by My Writers' Connection

Library of Congress Control Number: 2018965587
Paperback ISBN: 978-1-949595-14-7
Ebook ISBN: 978-1-949595-15-4

First Printing: February 2019

DEDICATION

I'd like to dedicate this book to my family near and far. Your unconditional love, support, and willingness to participate in my educational life is never ending.

To my husband, Josh, and our children, Tess and Jackson: Thank you for understanding my drive to contribute. I love the three of you beyond words.

CONTENTS

FOREWORD

By Beth Houf and Shelley Burgess

The life of an educational leader can be a lonely road. Your task list has multiplied, yet time seems to have diminished. It is essential that you have a strong network of support to celebrate the great things happening as well as get you through those rough moments. We wrote *Lead Like a PIRATE* to do just that. We wanted to help support educators by sharing our stories and strategies. We wanted to be sure that no one felt as if she or he was alone. Our goal has been to set up systems of support through our PLN to empower leaders to take risks to ensure that school is an amazing place . . . for both students and staff.

Since the book's release, it has been inspiring to watch our #LeadLAP crew grow. The examples and stories shared daily on our hashtag are inspiring beyond belief. What we came to realize is that we are surrounded by greatness that needed a voice. One evening after our book was published, we started brainstorming how we could continue to support leaders but in a way that wasn't the norm. One thing we discussed was that leaders sometimes get overwhelmed by the amount of information that is being shared at what seems like lightning speed. How might we offer bite-size expertise for leaders that would have a huge impact on schools? The *Lead Like a PIRATE Guides* were born.

As we work with educators around the globe, we have noticed that many believe leadership is for those with administrative roles. We feel very strongly that leading is an all-inclusive opportunity, no matter your position. As we write in *Lead Like a PIRATE*, people are less likely to tear down systems they help to build. How could we create a school where all identify as builders? We are honored to introduce our fourth of the *Lead Like a PIRATE Guides: Lead beyond Your Title: Creating Change in School from any Role* by Nili Bartley. Nili is a teacher and technology facilitator in Massachusetts who has brought to life the #LeadLAP mission of culture first, culture next, culture always from her role as educator and technology integration coach. The stories she shares show how true change can happen when you tap into the amazing strengths of *every* person in your school. Through the pages within this book, Nili's inspirational passion for making school an amazing place is evident through the strategies and examples that she shares.

As we write in *Lead Like a PIRATE*, PIRATE leadership is about being the kind of leaders we always wanted to be and creating the kinds of schools we dream of for kids. These leaders relentlessly search for ways to make school an amazing place. These leaders don't simply believe schools can be better; they *know* schools can be better and stop at nothing to make it happen. Nili Bartley is a PIRATE leader in every way, and we are honored to have her as part of our crew.

Lead Like a PIRATE

Passion

Pirate leaders bring their passion to work. They also work to identify and bring out the passions of their staff members and students.

Immersion

Pirate leaders are immersed in their work and relationships, which enables them to make an impact on those they lead.

Rapport

Pirate leaders intentionally build trust and rapport with the entire crew.

Ask and Analyze

Pirate leaders ask great questions and engage in meaningful conversations that empower people to take risks.

Transformation

Pirate leaders transform the mundane into the spectacular. They make essentials, such as staff meetings and professional development training, engaging and effective.

Enthusiasm

Pirate leaders are enthusiastic and positive. They work to create an environment where teachers and students are excited about coming to school each day.

MY STORY

It was a typical Monday afternoon staff meeting shortly after the 2014 Winter Break. A copy of the book *Teach Like a PIRATE* by Dave Burgess lay on the table in front of me, whispering words of confidence that only I could hear.

"Okay, anyone have anything to celebrate?" my principal asked as he kicked off the meeting. My hand shot up. Go time. "Yes, Nili?"

"Yeah, so I just wanted to announce that I've decided to become a PIRATE. If anyone would like to be a pirate with me, just like let me know. And here's the book if anyone wants to take a look." Polite smiles and blank stares hid thoughts of, *Oh, Nili*. Giggles bubbled around the room. But a few colleagues asked me about the book after the meeting, and we launched a mini book study. We were four strong. It felt very *Dead Poets Society*, which of course, made it cool. A few months later, when our Dead Poet Society PIRATE club unceremoniously disbanded, I realized that while I knew how to lead my students, leading my colleagues was another matter. Still, I held to my newly discovered PIRATE ways in the classroom and watched with delight as the level of enthusiasm in my classroom reached new heights. Of course it did not happen overnight. Along the way, I have heard all sorts of comments from both leaders and peers: "Sorry, PIRATE does not align with our writing initiative."

"Ha ha, what's your compass?" (And, my favorite) "I saw students running around the building wearing bandanas . . . I figured they were yours." I know now that those misperceptions (and the disbelief) about the PIRATE way of life came from a lack of understanding. I successfully refused to let those comments get in the way of creating amazing experiences for my students, but I *wish* I had taken greater responsibility for educating my colleagues and administrators. I had revolutionized my classroom but it was not until a few years later that I came to understand the power that we, as teachers, have to revolutionize *entire schools*, not just our own classrooms.

The most common titles in schools are students, educators, and administrators. You probably have a very clear picture of the role or responsibility that each one of these titles carries:

- **Educator**—a person who provides instruction or education; a teacher
- **Student**—a person who is studying at a school or college
- **Principal**—the person with the highest authority or most important position in an organization, institution, or group

Today, I know that everyone has the ability to lead change in schools. And if you find the courage to chart your own course and invite others on the journey, you might just surprise yourself when you discover your dream job and a freedom you may have never felt before.

In this book, I am going to challenge you to shake up the typical roles in education. I want you to look beyond titles and see how each person in your learning community—regardless of their age or position—can contribute in powerful ways. I want you to consider how you define your role and to ask how your students, colleagues, and administrators define their roles. Most importantly, think about how your school would look if each person was encouraged and equipped to lead from their strengths. Because the truth is each one of us can lead; in fact, we must.

PART ONE

SAILING INTO THE PIRATE WORLD WITH STUDENTS

Provide an uncommon
experience for your students,
and they will reward you with an
uncommon effort and attitude.

—Dave Burgess, *Teach Like a PIRATE*

Being a PIRATE will make
you take risks and get out of
your comfort zone. This will
change you, and then you
can change the world!

—Casey

EMBRACING THE PIRATE LIFE IN THE CLASSROOM

"Whatever it takes" is the mantra of PIRATE
leaders ready to make a difference.

–Shelley Burgess and Beth Houf, *Lead Like a PIRATE*

Mrs. Bartley taught in a unique way that
made school seem less like a chore
but more like an opportunity.

–Libby

My PIRATE journey began in the classroom in 2014. Inspired by my first ISTE conference and the "You Matter" session where I had met Angela Maiers, I had joined Twitter and was determined to be a connected educator. When school started that fall, a student asked me the question no one new to Twitter wants to answer: "Mrs. Bartley, how many Twitter followers do you have?"

I replied, "Well, it does not really matter how *many* you have as much as *who* it is that is following you. I have four."

But one of them was Angela Maiers, one of them was Beth Houf, and one of them was Jay Billy. The other was my husband.

My class and I quickly became hooked on Twitter. Any time my class did something I thought should be shared with the world, I tweeted about it. Any time someone responded, I projected the tweet on the whiteboard for students to see as soon as they walked in. We had started down the road to becoming a connected class, and my students were living it up.

And then we hit a bump. Well, it was a bit more than a bump; it was a full stop. A lesson I thought went quite well was called out as a complete flop by an observing administrator. I thought the lesson was different and fun. The kids loved it. My administrator did not. I was crushed. I began to question some of my work as an educator.

Thankfully, Beth Houf, whom I had taught beside early in my career and had continued to learn from through the years, knew me well enough to somehow understand that *Teach Like a PIRATE* might just do for me what it did for her: give me a one-of-a-kind opportunity to rediscover my *why*—and encourage me to live it. She mailed me a copy for my birthday in December of 2014. I read it cover to cover and made a conscious decision to become a PIRATE. I joined the ever-growing and supportive #TLAP crew online and even asked my colleagues to join me.

Then on the first day of school in 2015, I asked my students what every teacher should consider asking their students: "Who wants to be a PIRATE with me?"

After I explained what the PIRATE acronym meant for teachers and we discussed what it could mean for them as students, they jumped on board immediately. What fourth grader *doesn't* want to be a pirate? In the weeks and months that followed, they *owned* the role of PIRATES in our classroom and became leaders in their education.

We had a ritual of starting each morning with a positive chant. When we decided to become pirates together, I challenged my students to work in groups to come up with a PIRATE acronym to represent the kind of learning that would make them jump out of bed every morning and run to school. We combined the results from each group's PIRATE words to create a one-of-a-kind chant. For the remainder of the year, we used that chant to kick off every single morning, and we never had an *unPIRATEy* day again.

We, Crew 202, pledge to:

Participate,

Imagine,

Revolutionize our thinking,

Ask questions,

Take risks,

Engage, and Encourage!

We learn like pirates, hoo ha!

Hit the deck, hoo ha!

This is what we do here on Ship 202!

(bit.ly/PIRATEpledge)

From the first morning of our PIRATE adventure on, my students were *literally* running to get into our classroom (aka our "ship"). I loved hearing the quick footsteps coming down the hall. It was a race every day to see who would show up to Crew 202 first. A spirit of anticipation set the tone for the whole day.

Things changed in my classroom when we became PIRATE learners. We restarted sharing our accomplishments online—and never stopped. We looked forward to each day, and over time, every crew member in our classroom discovered they had something valuable to contribute to the class. In that way, every learner became a leader. And that was only the beginning!

Summary

There is nothing in the world like asking students to embrace an unconventional journey with you. The truth is, my brave students were not simply students anymore. They were PIRATE learners, and that meant something special to them. It meant when they came through our door, they were showing up to learn, stretch their thinking like never before, develop curiosity, accept new challenges, and help one another do the same. When they believed they were, in fact, more than their title of student, they sailed well beyond it. I witnessed their transformation happening right in front of me, and I realized that I was transforming as a teacher right along with them. We worked together as a crew. And whether you are teaming up with students, other staff members, or an online community of educators, and whether you joining them or they are joining you—or both—finding your crew is essential; in fact, it changes everything.

Leadership Treasure Hunt
(Find This)

Take a minute (or several) to think about whether you are alone in your educational journey. What can you do about it? Who might you join? Who might join you?

Navigating the Seas
(Think about This)

Are you and your students (or staff) sailing together as a crew? Have you ever given your students (or staff) the opportunity to express what the best learning/teaching in the world looks like to them? The "stuff" that would get them literally running in? It is time!

Charting the Course
(Take Action)

Start asking yourself who your crewmates are, what you are doing to make an impact, and what your next steps might be together. Ask them what it is they want to run back to every single day, and do one thing tomorrow to help make that happen.

Connecting to the World, Connecting to Each Other

Hi, chat's in 90 minutes right??
36 minutes!
25 minutes!
15 minutes!
11 minutes!
I am in Spain right now, and it is actually 1:40
in the morning, but I really don't care.

—several students eager for a chat to start
(This particular chat was in the summer.)

I never anticipated that connecting and sharing with other educators and classes around the world would connect us so deeply as a class. As connecting became a part of our culture, I realized that my crew was bonding over our incredible experiences. The feedback we received from sharing our work and ideas inspired my students to reach for more.

One of the things we began doing more frequently was to use our connection with rock-star educators to learn as much as we possibly could about them as change makers. What we did not realize was that each interview would push us closer and closer to becoming change makers ourselves. We invited Dave and Shelley Burgess, Paul Solarz, Angela Maiers, Lourds Lane, directors of professional learning at BrainPOP, an educational platform based on short animated movies (and even the voice of BrainPOP's own Tim!), the CEOs of Ideaphora, and local heroes into our classroom for virtual and in-person interviews.

Together, we prepped for the interviews by learning about the people who would be our guests. We watched a video, for example, of Dave Burgess using his magic during a keynote presentation. From there, we brainstormed questions that we wanted to ask. On the day of the interview, students took different roles, managing the technology, asking questions, and interacting with our guest. They loved taking charge, and they loved connecting face to face with the people we had been communicating with online.

Another experience I brought into the classroom was something that had been a huge benefit to me in my personal PIRATE journey. After participating in a few Twitter chats—which I found fun and enlightening—I wondered, *Why shouldn't my students feel the adrenaline rush of sharing ideas and supporting each other in a chat?*

Of course, my fourth-grade students were not on Twitter individually (we used my account for the class), so we tested the chat experience using a backchanneling tool to share our New Year's resolutions with one another. As students typed, no one made a sound, but there were smiles all around the room. We shared our personal and classroom PIRATE goals for the year, and I remember thinking, *this was something special.* I knew somehow that the experience was just the beginning of what would be perhaps one of the most important things we would do as a class.

Chats proved valuable to our class because even my most introverted students could freely express themselves in writing. Every student had a voice, and we learned that even a silent conversation can change someone's life.

Next we tried Edmodo, a community building platform for students and teachers. Through Edmodo, we were able to connect more similarly to a Twitter chat. I was able to see my students demonstrate immense support and empathy for one another as they answered questions on a variety of topics. This was such a powerful discovery that I decided to do something completely crazy and assign "chatting" for homework. If students could join in real time, they did, and those who could not posted answers later that night or the next day. They "said" hellos, goodbyes, and even confided personal feelings. They commented on each other's posts, "liked" them, and sparked real conversations with each other.

> Even a silent conversation can change someone's life.

A few weeks later, we took the level of interaction up a notch by inviting Beth Houf to chat with us to talk about being PIRATEs. She shared that since becoming a PIRATE, "I have learned that it is okay to take risks and try new things. We do not have to do things the way we have always done them! ENTHUSIASM and PASSION are an important part of learning for sure!" And the floodgates opened!

Twenty minutes passed in no time as students shared what being a PIRATE meant to them. I absolutely love what one student, Maura, shared during the chat:

> I have taken more risks, tried my absolute best, found things I'm passionate about, encouraged others, participated, have been adventurous, and I am even more excited to wake up and come to school every day!

From then on, we held regular chats—amongst ourselves and with guests. Connecting to one another in this fast-paced and authentic digital environment lets students share their thoughts. They are able to initiate questions and respond to others' questions and ideas.

Each time we wrapped up a chat, I signed off the same way: "Good night, Crew 202! Once again, we sailed into an amazing and inspiring chat that we will revisit tomorrow! And now it's time to sail out. :) Your very inspired captain."

As much as I hoped to inspire my students, they inspired and encouraged me every day. In that way, they were leaders *to me*.

Summary

Connecting with one another and with leaders in education became a significant part of our culture. It showed students they were not only good enough to connect with people who were making a difference in the world but gave them the confidence to do the same. Make it easy on yourself. Start by asking one person with whom you are already connected to be a guest on a Skype call, Google Hangout, or chat. Focus on the first experience, make it count, and make it good. Before you know it, your students and staff will take it to the next level, and I predict you will see incredible results.

Leadership Treasure Hunt
(Find This)

Look for opportunities where you can jump into online conversations. Perhaps your school or district has a hashtag and hosts a chat once a month. The impact you could bring to your school or classroom is too good not to taste. Not only will you be learning and growing in education, but you will be bringing the power of a chat back to your people. In my experience, even our very youngest students crave to connect.

Navigating the Seas
(Think about This)

How often do you encourage online connection for your students and/or staff? How might you like to? Which platform might you start with?

Charting the Course
(Take Action)

Create an opportunity for your staff and/or students to connect through an online conversation that gets them thinking deeply and sharing with each other. Do not be afraid to go for the unconventional! Once you get comfortable, let one of them take the lead!

Share your thoughts and ideas!
#LeadLAP

DISCOVERING THE STUDENT EDCAMP EXPERIENCE

When students put their phones in their lockers for the day and are asked to learn what we tell them they must learn, engagement immediately drops, no matter how good a teacher we think we are.

—Joy Kirr, *Shift This!*

By the third month of our PIRATE adventure, my fourth graders were constantly inspiring me to go beyond the teacher I was to become the teacher I wanted to be. That happened largely because they knew they each had a voice and that I was listening—hard. And this is what I heard:

Give us something that counts.

We want to change the world.

We have ideas.

We love technology, so BRING IT!

We are willing to take risks.

We believe everyone matters.

We want to keep connecting globally.

We want to learn.

We CAN do this.

On a not-so-beautiful New England morning in March 2015, I had the unforgettable experience of going to an Edcamp. I was leading a PIRATE session and felt so incredibly nervous as I looked out at a packed room. Fortunately, my energy and enthusiasm took over, and before attendees knew it, I was chanting the Crew 202 PIRATE Pledge, hoo ha'ing, and hitting the floor.

I explained that being a PIRATE was a mindset, shared how things had changed in my classroom, and even heard from a few other PIRATEs in the crowd. When the Edcamp concluded, I knew I could officially call myself a PIRATE educator. I walked away from that event thinking, *This is great! I can give my students an Edcamp experience, and it will be like nothing they've ever done before. They will lead, and they will be heard.*

Completely pumped to take Edcamp to the classroom, I did just that. Although we did not actually launch our big event until a month later, we certainly set the stage. Every day, I hyped up "Crew 202 Edcamp" as *the* day of school students would not want to miss. I also took time to get students thinking about potential Edcamp sessions they either wanted to facilitate in order to explore a topic or lead in order to share a topic they felt they knew well. We held several discussions during our morning meetings to model appropriate topics within education as well as to practice what an Edcamp conversation might look like. We discussed the structure and expectations and wrote them down in preparation for the big day. Thirty-minute, highly interactive sessions led by students happening at the same time would be new for all of us. Like Edcamp for educators, I wanted students to feel confident, yet unlike the Edcamp I had attended, I took the same-day pressure off. Students could certainly choose topics together (as can educators), and before I knew it, we not only had a poster of topics students wanted to lead or facilitate but also assurance that enough students would attend each session. Once our schedule was finally up and ready to go, the excitement in the air was contagious, and the message was loud and clear: No preparation is necessary. Just bring your passion, voice, and ears.

During the couple of hours dedicated solely to Crew 202 Edcamp, I gained tremendous knowledge as a student participant right alongside my "classmates." Conversations centered around the calmness in drawing and the power of creating with our hands. Students discovered the world of app smashing, developed ideas for global learning, brainstormed student-led digital chat topics, and critically discussed the status of our school lunches and required homework. They talked about their experiences with animals, recess, sports, brain breaks, synergy in the classroom, bouncy-ball chairs, and the effects of positive thinking. A few leaders acted on impulse and asked to use LEGO bricks, scissors, paper, laptops, and more to make learning even more meaningful with those they were teaching.

Watching my students that day, I witnessed courage, leadership, and empathy. What more could a teacher, or the world for that matter, ask for? Students encouraged each other and showed a genuine interest in each conversation. They learned about their classmates, and they learned about themselves. Some of my quietest students spoke loudly with confidence as they shared what mattered most to them, and many times it was my most vocal students who quietly supported them.

> Watching my students that day, I witnessed courage, leadership, and empathy. What more could a teacher, or the world for that matter, ask for?

Even students who were in and out of the classroom showed off their talents as their classmates ate up every second. While one drew pictures that helped us tap into his personality, another student called for volunteers to help demonstrate his daily strengthening exercises. The bottom line is my students and I played a variety of roles and had a chance to see who we are in each of them. And together, we created something successful.

I know other teachers leave Edcamps with the same thought and motivation to bring the idea of peer-led learning back to their classrooms. What unfolded with my very own crew of twenty-four PIRATE students ignited a commitment to Edcamp for myself, my students, and later for my colleagues. Today the #studentedcamp movement is thriving, and I am honored to be part of it.

Summary

We have no excuse for not providing choice, voice, and passion in the classroom. Student Edcamps are a perfect way to show students (and you, and whoever is watching!) that you place student-led learning high on your priority list. It is this type of learning that students crave and that they will need to be successful in the future. So do not wait! Jump on the student Edcamp bandwagon today!

Leadership Treasure Hunt
(Find This)

Look for an opportunity to bring Edcamp to students. Maybe you are an administrator and you know the perfect class ready to pilot it. Or maybe you are a teacher and you have experienced Edcamp yourself but have not yet considered trying it with students. Pick a time to make it your own and go for it.

Navigating the Seas
(Think about This)

How well do you know the students in your classroom or building? How often do you listen to their hearts, their passions, what *they* want? How do you make time for experiences like Edcamp? What can you do to make time for them? For administrators, there is a whole chapter on this later in the book.

Charting the Course
(Take Action)

Ask your students and/or staff what *they* want to learn and carve out even just one hour. Hand them an Edcamp experience and become the student. You will not regret it. If you are looking to bring Edcamp style PD to staff, be sure to read the chapter devoted to just that toward the end of the book.

Share your thoughts and ideas!
#LeadLAP

UNLEASHING OUR STUDENTS' PASSIONS

Everyone wins when highly effective leaders
bring their passion to work.

—Shelley Burgess and Beth Houf, *Lead Like a PIRATE*

Educating the mind without educating
the heart is no education at all.

—Aristotle

Done right, innovation can work with the Common Core
and allow freedom in the teacher's approach as well
as in the students' learning choices.

—Don Wettrick, *Pure Genius*

The teacher has to be more active in this learning experience than anything else. Because students need coaching.
They need to be connected to the right resources, to the
right people. They need help on their projects. There are
going to be pitfalls and failures, and they need someone
there to kind of say, that's okay, that's what it's all about.

—A.J. Juliani, coauthor of *LAUNCH* discussing 20% time

After reading *Teach Like a PIRATE*, I picked up *Pure Genius* by Don Wettrick—and I was instantly hooked. I had done service-learning projects with students for years, and they were always the most memorable because the work my students did during these projects mattered. So when I learned about how Wettrick used Genius Hour and innovation classes to make learning meaningful for his students on an ongoing basis, I was all-in. Committed to adapting this adventure for my students, we came up with our own Genius Hour name: *Just QLICC* (Question, Learn, Inform by Creating, and Change the World). The acronym, which sounds like *click,* reminded us that we were dedicated to using technology with the purpose of changing the world. And of course, we created a chant (bit.ly/JustQLICC) to kick off every Just QLICC period.

Casey, a student, created this infographic for Just QLICC

We were dedicated to using technology with the purpose of changing the world.

At first, our Just QLICC time took place every Wednesday afternoon. But as we neared the end of the school year, we found more time to devote to our innovative projects. When we launched this new element of our work, the greatest challenge was helping my fourth graders understand that the project they chose had to in some way change the world. Being a world changer is a difficult concept to grasp—even for me. We had many discussions, in groups and one on one as we thought about *how* we could change the world. What I reiterated to my curious students was that anything we could do from sending clean water to Africa to writing an ABC book for first graders was making a difference for at least one person (or animal or community). In our own unique way, we would make a difference.

Another challenge was identifying our problem-solving passions. To be passionate about sports, music, reading, technology, or even taking care of animals is common amongst fourth graders, but the twist was figuring out what we saw that we wanted to change in the world. In order to help students through this process, I showed them videos of students just like them discussing local and global issues they were involved in. I also did something very simple. I gave them time to explore, read, and talk about anything they came across that jumped out at them. It was also important for students to know that they could use other passions (and strengths) to help them create something awesome for the world to see.

The requirements for the first Just QLICC project were reasonable but challenging:

- Students were required to present their research and ideas.
- They had to create a simulation and either a prototype or a book or website.

And in addition, they needed to tie in a famous African American's inspiration. (This was not an easy assignment!)

We increased the stakes by inviting parents and teachers to a special presentation on June 4. I grew increasingly nervous as the presentation date drew near, but I knew deep down that regardless of the outcome, we were doing something special that our school had never seen before. After all, when a ten-year-old student creates a 3D prototype for a solar-powered blanket in the hopes of helping the homeless, you know you have encouraged innovation. When another student shows up with a parakeet persuading her listeners that birds should

be used as therapeutic animals, you know you have promoted "no box" thinking. And when two students join forces to create their own official book donation organization because they firmly believe every human should have a book, you know you have played an important role in encouraging the next generation to be good people.

When June 4 finally arrived, seeing the result of all their hard work, imagination, and persistence made for one of best moments in my teaching career. My students spoke and presented like experts, convincing their parents the real-world issues they had so passionately researched were worth paying attention to. Parents were awestruck by the knowledge, confidence, and empowerment they had just witnessed. I knew I had succeeded in creating a class of leaders.

For the next two weeks, families took action. Students collected hundreds of books, several items for greyhounds, and pledges to plant vegetables for food pantries were collected. They also raised over $1,000 to be split amongst several organizations, including the Imagination Foundation sparked by Caine's Arcade so that schools everywhere could be touched by innovation and creativity. Students would soon invite several classrooms to play the arcade games they created, which allowed them to raise even more money for the Imagination Foundation.

Summary

When we step back and let students (and staff) explore their passions and take action on things that are meaningful to them, they will come up with ideas and solutions beyond our imagination. Regardless of what you call the time, make sure you are giving students and staff opportunities to learn about their passions. And when you are ready, go past passion. Push each individual to contribute something, to give their passion a purpose, and enjoy the ride. When empowered people are driving, and especially when they have an audience, their distance has no limit.

Leadership Treasure Hunt
(Find This)

Find time in the day, week, month, or year to bring "genius" time to students or staff. Shift things around. Eliminate something from the schedule if you need to; the benefits of this "passion time" will far outweigh any risk you take when something else gets the boot.

Navigating the Seas
(Think about This)

How are you allowing for students and/or staff to discover their passions? How are they consistently learning more about them? What actions are you encouraging them to take?

Charting the Course
(Take Action)

Implement your own "genius time" that makes sense for your students and/or staff. You can do it! Remember to buckle up, enjoy the ride, and guide your students and/or staff to be the change-making individuals they can be!

Share your thoughts and ideas!
#LeadLAP

Unlocking the Strengths in Our Students

Be relentless in seeking out and
nurturing each person's greatness.

—Shelley Burgess and Beth Houf, *Lead Like a PIRATE*

Taking time to find the strengths of individuals
is not an expenditure but an investment that
can come in copious amounts of growth.

—George Couros

As teachers, your greatest power comes from knowing
your students. A personal understanding of knowing
your students empowers you to design learning experiences that connect students with their passions and
strengths to help them find their place in the world.

—Katie Martin

Discovering our passions was a leading factor in our "genius" success, but there was another critical element that sparked powerful change in our classroom: finding our strengths. Please join me in traveling back to April when we were sailing strong on our PIRATE journey. Things were going great! Crew 202 thrived as we threw ourselves into Just QLICC every second we could. Then, just when I thought the learning could not possibly get better, *Learn Like a PIRATE* by Paul Solarz arrived in the mail. I dove in, hungry to know if and how I could take my students to the next level of PIRATE. Within a month, they were opening and closing end-of-day discussions, respecting each other's style of leading the class, and on their way to running a whole day of school from beginning to end.

This commitment to a stronger student-led classroom pushed me to take a look at the SuperYou FUNdation curriculum. A parent brought to my attention the fact that I could launch a unique experience in the classroom. I reviewed a brand-new curriculum that was created with the goal of increasing empathy. What I discovered was that Lourds Lane, a writer and musician, had developed lessons right up my passion alley. The curriculum is based on the arts as well as components of social emotional learning and character education. I was intrigued by the possibility of bringing lessons to my students that would challenge them to connect to their inner superhero as well as identify their "superpowers" in what appeared to be a fun way to learn.

Immediately drawn to Lourds' original song, "I am a superhero," my PIRATE learners and I decided together to give a few of her lessons a shot. They are full of art, music, poetry, and reflection. I noticed my students not only tapping into their superpowers but literally jumping up and down with excitement. We were already PIRATES, but now we each held a power in our pocket, which would allow us all to reach our potential in new ways.

Whether it was calmness, kindness, humor, intellect, hope, creativity, or perseverance, each of us claimed our strengths. We also became completely vulnerable. I allowed my students to see me. Instead of only seeing a happy teacher who took risks, my students saw me struggle to admit I was not using courage in every situation in life, yet I deeply wanted to. This gave my students permission to not only become just as vulnerable but to call on each other for help. And they did. They led each other (and me) during every lesson. Discovering what we brought to the table and also what we wished for was no independent journey. We were a team.

> **Whether it was calmness, kindness, humor, intellect, hope, creativity, or perseverance, each of us claimed our strengths. We also became completely vulnerable.**

Because students were able to dig into their learning beyond traditional academic areas, they saw each other differently, gained more respect for one another, and had a whole lot of fun in the process. Confidence spread like fire across all subject areas, attendance was off the charts, and calling each other by our new superhero names became the norm. In fact, when students soon created rubrics for projects in the classroom, "Did I use my superpower?" was an expected column not because I asked but because they held themselves to bringing it— every single day.

Here are a few ideas to help you unleash the strengths—or their superpowers, as the SuperPIRATES of Crew 202 say—of your students and staff.

Include Those You Serve in Decisions

Especially the big ones, especially those that make you hesitant. Bring ideas to your people and let them help you decide. I have learned many gems from educator and author Angela Watson, and one is that even the most innovative ideas must be right for the people in front of you in that moment. Somehow, I valued this before I heard her speak at *Tomorrow's Classrooms Today* two years later. I brought SuperYou to my students first, and I honored their voices. Yet in full PIRATE style, they jumped at the idea. I was a little hesitant as we were already PIRATES. To no surprise, they immediately came up with a declaration I will never forget. "We'll be SuperPIRATES!"

Invest Time in Researching Strength (and Passion!) Based Lessons and Platforms

Check Out the SuperYou FUNdation

There are really no words that can adequately describe what Lourds Lane and SuperYou were able to do for my students (and me), so I advise you to check it out at www.superyoufun.org. What is truly amazing is that every classroom and school that has embraced the curriculum has done so with amazing buy-in from teachers and administrators! In fact, it is common to see parents in capes unleashing what makes them special too! The combination of music and empowerment makes it impossible to resist the urge to jump right in.

Check Out Thrively

Thrively.com is a one-of-a-kind interactive platform that allows students of all ages to launch a journey of self-discovery based on their strengths and passions. If you have not enrolled your students (And teachers!), do not wait. It is just that good. When I received a strength profile that included "gift of gab" and "remarkable athleticism," I was so all-in; I created a roster that night and needless to say, my kiddos jumped on the very next morning. To learn more about my students' experience with Thrively in helping them unleash their strengths and passions, please visit a post I wrote a few years ago. (bit.ly/THRIVELY)

Check Out Ignite Your S.H.I.N.E.®

If you do not know LaVonna Roth's work, put this book down right now and follow her on Twitter. She is on a mission to increase empathy and decrease bullying. Luckily for the teachers and students I worked with over the past couple of years, her Ignite Your S.H.I.N.E. lessons became available on Thrively just in time for "Genius Hour." Through her videos and journal prompts, LaVonna transforms into a teacher for every student through a series of online lessons. She does not simply share the power of combining our strengths and passions but communicates the opportunity every child and teacher has in making the world better when we learn to S.H.I.N.E. To learn more about students' experiences with these powerful lessons (from the voices of students!), please visit a post I wrote a couple of years ago. (bit.ly/igniteyourshine)

Learn from Principals Who Infuse "Superpowers" into Their Culture

Jay Billy owns a cape as well as a Superman hat. He knows who he is and leads by example to encourage others to share who they are. When Lourds Lane and SuperYou came to Slackwood School, he knew "superpower" would be infused into the culture of his building and that every teacher and student would have a chance to show off what makes them unique. He still speaks of this day with indescribable energy. Brenda Maurao has been a mentor and friend over the past couple of years. When she became principal at Stall Brook Elementary School in Bellingham, MA, she made it her mission to unleash the superpowers in both her students and staff to boost achievement. In fact, everything at Stall Brook is "super," and this mindset she has embedded is making an impact. Follow Jay, Brenda, and other leaders like them; reach out, and learn from those unleashing the strengths of their students and staff every single day.

Model Your Personal Journey

I experienced every SuperYou lesson right along with my students. In fact, I would soon be spending a weekend creating BrainPOP PD with an amazing group of educators in New York City, and I knew no one! What a perfect opportunity to bring courage in my pocket, use it, and report back to my students. This is exactly what I did. If you want students (and staff!) to get personal, you need to get personal first and share the moments when you unleash the strengths you have and, most certainly, those you do not quite have yet but deeply desire.

Encourage Collaboration Even During Self-Discovery!

I am not the one who chose my superhero name; my students did. They chose Lioness because it was courage I chose as my "wish superpower" and PIRATE for obvious reasons. When they chose Lioness PIRATE, it gave them permission to help each other with their own superhero names. This was invaluable. Whether you ask students to identify their strengths, "genius," superpowers, or gifts, let them help one another in the process. There is no better way for them to learn about their peers! Now imagine throwing the question "What makes you so unique?" out to teachers AND having them help each other brainstorm answers. I am not sure there is anything more powerful.

Launch Strengths- and Passion-Based Introductions

I piloted with a group of third graders creating videos for their fourth-grade teachers. The videos explained a strength they could bring to the classroom to help themselves and others, a topic they are passionate about learning, and an area they would like help with. Fourth-grade teachers went nuts when they saw these videos arrive from their incoming students before they even met! Too often student voices are missing in the placement process. Be the one who includes them in your school and encourage colleagues to follow your lead! But do not stop there! Create one for your students based on your strengths and passions and encourage your colleagues and administrators to do the same!

See the Person, Not the Job

If we want students to tap into their strengths, we must as leaders tap into the strengths of our colleagues, and administrators must tap into the strengths of their teachers. It is all about modeling. In *The Innovator's Mindset*, George Couros (in addition to the many countless gems in that amazing book) discusses a superintendent he once worked with by the name of Kelly Wilkins. Kelly created a position she knew would utilize his strengths and told him this: "We do not fit people into jobs. We find the best people and fit the jobs to them." This resonated with me. I hope it resonates with you for all of the work you do with every single person you serve.

Set up Compass Points: Best Ice Breaker Ever!

This amazing activity from the National School Reform Faculty can be used with staff (or why not students!) and is described beautifully in *Learner-Centered Innovation* by Katie Martin. You can also modify it as Lourds Lane and I did to kick things off at an all-day PD experience. (We had educators identify with famous superheroes, and it was an absolute blast!) The premise is that people are asked to identify their leading style: visionary, empathetic, analyzes the details, or action oriented. They meet in groups and list together their strengths, challenges, the group they feel is the hardest to work with, what other groups need to know about their style, and what they value about the other groups. When we did this in real time, it blew us away. For the rest of the day, everyone worked incredibly well together, opened up, became vulnerable, asked for help, and beyond anything, else were encouraged to shine.

Summary

We all need "jump up and down" lessons, so if you are teaching with your feet stuck to the floor, you are missing out! As Angela Watson says, *"Eliminate the good to make time for the best."* I believe Crew 202 was doing just that. Whether it falls on your lap or you go get it, bring the innovative lessons and approaches to those you serve. Let them be part of the decision-making process. Dive in together. Keep in mind as you take teaching and learning to new levels, the importance of unleashing the superpowers of everyone around you. In the process, work on discovering and sharing your own superpowers too!

Leadership Treasure Hunt
(Find This)

Look at your students, colleagues, and administrators. How excited is everyone about learning? What is it that they are spending most of their time learning about? If you are struggling to find enough moments in your building that allow you to learn about yourself, colleagues and administrators to learn about themselves, and most importantly students, to learn about who they are, be the one to spark the change.

Navigating the Seas
(Think about This)

How often does your heart race while you're teaching? How often do your students' hearts race? Using cutting-edge teaching methods challenges you as an educator and helps create those "jump up and down" moments for your students.

Charting the Course
(Take Action)

Whether it is for students or staff, find a "jump up and down" lesson or learning approach or create one and have a blast. Go after the life-changing stuff, not the test-prep lessons or those driven by compliance. We live on a planet that needs our kids to become people who think, feel, and love. In my experience, the best way to get them there is to help students (and staff!) figure out who they are, who they can become, and what they have to offer.

Share your thoughts and ideas!
#LeadLAP

PASSING THE MIC

People are less likely to tear down
systems they help build.

–Shelley Burgess and Beth Houf, *Lead Like a PIRATE*

As the days went on, it didn't seem like school
anymore. It seemed like hanging out with our new
family. It's crazy, how in the beginning of fourth
grade, we just made this simple goal of having the
'Best Year Ever,' and literally, we had the best year
ever! It became something bigger than us.

–Casey

Back in September, we had set out to have the "best year ever" and those three words stayed on the board until the last second of the last day of school. As I think fondly of my SuperPIRATES, I realize that because of our dedication to "best year ever," we learned together to embrace everything, good and not so good. We feared that, if we did not, we might miss out on something life-changing. My students became hungry for inspiration as well as the chance to inspire. At the end of the year, they were certainly given a huge opportunity to do both, and we took full advantage.

As one of the first classes in the world to dive into her "superhero" lessons, we interested Lourds Lane. She wanted to immerse herself in our journey. She is a prodigy violinist, performing artist, and creator of a Broadway-bound musical. I immediately said "YES" to her offer of coming to our school. For my students, the countdown was on as they saw Lourds as another PIRATE educator leading by example, yet one they would get to meet beyond a video call. June 14–16 were the new hyped-up dates, the days of school not to be missed by anyone.

We knew we would be preparing for a superhero show the whole school would be watching, but we did not quite know what to expect. Yet in three short days, my students and I were somehow ready to empower an audience of six hundred people. Quiet students shared their voices. Shy students grabbed the spotlight. Every student played a significant but different role. From breakdancing to backflips and artwork to creative skits oozing with personality, each act exploded with courage, humor, and camaraderie.

It was not easy. Lourds had put students in situations every moment of each day where they were forced to think on their feet, collaborate, problem solve, sweat, and persevere. Even I felt out of my element, at times, as I am not accustomed to the performing-arts world and intense level of commitment required to survive it. As their leader, however, I passed the mic to Lourds, and the results were invaluable.

We had joined forces to create a new mindset for my students. They were able to see themselves as individuals who soaked up inspiration but who could also get up, take the stage, and inspire. The positive reaction from our staff, students, and their families overwhelmed me. Students in other classrooms ran home that superhero day exploding with news about what they had just witnessed in our gym, something our school had never seen before. Through their experience in the spotlight, their dance video, and willingness to share their voices, my students ended up inspiring everyone around them to find their special superpowers.

After this experience, students reported using their superpowers to get through everything from social and emotional situations

> My students ended up inspiring everyone around them to find their special superpowers.

to academic and physical challenges. In fact, after running a 5K soon after, two of my SuperPIRATES came sprinting up to me screaming how they had just used their superpowers to help them finish. One student used perseverance to help her keep going, and the other used creativity to think of a way to encourage herself to keep running. They were proud. They had dug deep and conquered something they otherwise may not have.

One of the most important leadership lessons I learned during our PIRATE journey that first year was the value of passing the mic—how to give control to my students, why it was essential to let people in, and what to do (or not) to encourage others to jump in and take the lead. Here are a few ways you can do that:

Let Others In

Whether your students become PIRATE learners or discover their inner superhero (or maybe both!), it is close to impossible to encourage leadership alone. Let others in. My students would not be who they are today without the influence of the educators, business experts, parents, and community members we let into our classroom (both by video and in real life). These leaders talked with my students, invested time in their lives, and sparked confidence in them. If you are an administrator promoting leadership for your teachers, do the same for them! All will reap the benefits.

"Give Me Five"

Just three words and one brilliant concept helped pave the way for individual leadership journeys and, at the same time, brought students together. "Give Me Five" is a practice I picked up from *Learn Like a PIRATE* that taught my students to step into their confidence and support one another. No matter what we were doing, I encouraged my students to stand up and say "Give me five" when they had a relevant insight or idea that might be helpful to their classmates. It took some practice, but by the end of the school year, my students had mastered appropriate times to use this powerful student-owned strategy. They also supported their classmates when they asked for five; they ached for their peers to feel the sense of victory in getting the class's attention for an important purpose. Witnessing how this was bringing them together was enough good to last a lifetime. So bring *Give me Five* to your students (and staff!). Especially with younger kiddos, I recommend having everyone trace their hand and create colorful *Give me Five* sticks. This way when a student calls one, all classmates are involved. No matter what they are doing, they drop everything, grab their Give me Five stick, and hold it up to honor the student who was brave enough to call one.

Earn a Silent Day

Another tactic I picked up from Paul Solarz's book was allowing students to earn a "Silent Day" during which I did not say a word. This practice was one of the best educational decisions I have ever made. On my Silent Day, I wore a sticky note that said, "Sorry, I can't talk today." That means I could not answer questions or give directions. Learning is truly led by the students—all day.

If you do a Silent Day, all of the leadership skills you have been instilling in your students will come to life, and their level of engagement and responsibility will knock your socks off. Students need to practice leading. Silent Day is the perfect opportunity to let them show you they are capable of doing so.

If you are an administrator, imagine bringing "Silent Day" to your whole school. You might be nervous that teachers and students might not step it up, but what if they do?

Host a Cardboard Arcade

If you have not learned of Caine's Arcade, have a box of tissues ready. I brought Caine's first video to my students, wiped tears while watching (I still do to this day!), and could not say "no" when my students asked to do their own. To truly own their creations and provide an audience, I knew students would need to do more than build the arcade. They would need to host it. To celebrate our Just QLICC mission, students invited other classrooms to buy tickets and play, launched their designs (after several revisions), and collected money for the Imagination Foundation. As I watched students and teachers from other classrooms play the games my students had so thoughtfully built, it was mind boggling to me the level of creativity, empathy, and leadership erupting from my special crew. In that moment, I stared at them in disbelief and thought, *I may have just reached a new level of leadership.* I sat back, became the official raffle-ticket ripper, and smiled for the rest of the morning.

Encourage Pride in Your Theme(s)

Perhaps the most beautiful part of our arcade was that my SuperPIRATES stayed true to their name and created games with either a superhero or PIRATE theme. Looking at the colorful signs they created to tell the world who they are, I was so proud to just be a part of it. Whatever your themes for the year, let your students and staff run with them, create art representing them, sing songs that resonate with pride, and do whatever it takes for them to believe they are capable leaders in their journeys.

Make "Awesome" a Public Announcement

Perhaps the most moving scene of our superhero show was when students passed the mic to each other as they declared their superhero names, their superpowers, and how they are going to change the world. This "call and response" moment was monumental as every child and adult in the audience affirmed each student's declaration. As if the show was not enough, students became the stars of a one-of-a-kind superhero music video you can check out here! (bit.ly/Iamasuperhero) You can also view video interviews here with students sharing the power in discovering who they are in addition to interviews with many of their parents AND some of my former colleagues! (bit.ly/SuperYouFUN) In whatever capacity makes sense for you, encourage students (and staff!) to announce their awesomeness. Make sure the crowd is cheering.

Summary

To be an effective leader, we must pass the mic and let others in. My students learned from so many people. They also learned to open their hearts and minds, and as a result, they opened themselves up to learning from each other. It is okay to embrace something no one else knows about, no matter how different it is. In fact, sometimes it is the unconventional ideas (like PIRATES revolutionizing education or a musician teaching kids that they are all, in fact, superheroes) that make the biggest impact. So set your goals high, share them with the world, and invite others to help lead the way.

Leadership Treasure Hunt
(Find This)

Go out of your way to connect to other educators and look for the unconventional that strikes you as something that might just make sense for you and your crew.

Navigating the Seas
(Think about This)

What have you embraced with your students and or staff that few (or none) have done before? What are you waiting for? What might be holding you back?

Charting the Course
(Take Action)

I dare you to try something new that you and your students and/or staff believe in—even if no one else is doing anything like it. Although you may sense judgment or doubt, the energy your crew and you will feel may just make you want to dance!

PIRATE Students Share the Impact of Their Fourth-Grade Journey—Three Years Later

Fourth grade was the most empowering, awesome, staggering experience of my elementary career. Being a SuperPIRATE of Crew 202 was great. I love the program (SuperYou FUNdation) because it takes life skills, like being confident and loving yourself, and teaches them to kids. There were no boring lectures. It was hands-on learning, not sit-in-your-seat learning. This program lets kids express themselves in their own unique way. That made the students really happy. I know it made me extra happy because it made me feel comfortable in the classroom. With all the other kids expressing themselves, I did not feel alone and scared. I felt happy and safe!

—Luke (aka Mr. Kindness)

Whenever someone asks me if fourth grade was a good year, the answer is always simple: Yes. It's not just because some of my best friends were in that class, but it's because of what we learned and how we learned it. Instead of the typical teacher-teaches-student setup, Mrs. Bartley let us teach each other. I changed in fourth grade. I came out of my shell, and I became more confident. I made great new friends—two of whom are my best friends still. I learned to like math. Fourth grade was the first year that I was taught stuff in interesting ways—not just reading out of a textbook. Now, math is my favorite subject.

—Jordyn

Where do I begin? My fourth-grade year was definitely a year I could not forget. Being a part of Crew 202 really has made an impact on who I am today. It inspired me to really be who I am and to embrace all of my feelings and everything I have to share. It was such a great year for me, and I loved the whole experience of becoming a member of Crew 202. It was so fun to be able to have an experience with things such as skyping BrainPOP. A second great memory was when we became superheroes and met Lourds Lane and embraced our true personalities. I loved being able to work with all my friends and collaborate on things such as BrainPOP activities together and having a great time every day with the crew and amazing captain.

—Kyle

PART TWO

DIVING INTO DEEPER WATERS

We All Play a Role in Leading Our Schools

It's not supposed to be easy—
it's supposed to be worth it.

—Dave Burgess

I had taken a seat at our first-day staff assembly and was looking forward to discussing professional learning communities. I was (and still am!) passionate about ideas like taking responsibility for all of the kids in our schools—not just our own students—using our strengths to help them, having productive conversations with colleagues, and feeling a sense of togetherness. I was beaming with excitement as we found a seat when I suddenly heard a voice close by. "Nili, don't you dare say a word. It's just one more thing." Excitement squashed.

This astonishingly common pattern of behavior, I believe, is why at the same moment I declared piracy, I was only scratching the surface of a wall that for many teachers took years of building. I have felt this wall go up many times, one that resists new ideas and approaches. For many, it is almost automatic because it has been building for years. What is striking to me is that more often than not, our students do not see a wall for themselves. I can only truly speak for the elementary levels, but students typically buy in when we present something new. In fact, their excitement is typically off the charts.

Students typically buy in when we present something new. In fact, their excitement is typically off the charts.

Sure, our students do not have years of experience influencing them, nor do they have the demands on them teachers do, but I also think their excitement comes from viewing new opportunities enthusiastically by nature. They absorb whatever energy we bring to the classroom. If you are like me, maybe you can identify more with your students in that regard than with some of your peers. If you love to learn and share new things and get excited about striving for unconventional learning—maybe *you* are a PIRATE educator too. I hope so!

In this next section, we are going to move beyond the classroom and look at ways that we can use the PIRATE educator mindset to lead our schools. When we allow *passion, immersion, asking* and *analyzing, transformation,* and *enthusiasm* to guide us, we'll stop seeing walls and start seeing new waters to sail. Yes, there are occasional waves, sometimes storms, but never walls. When our *why,* fortified with a PIRATE mentality, drives us, even the constraints, stress, and clouds of standardized testing will not be able to stop us from creating amazing learning and leading experiences for *all* students.

When we become PIRATE leaders, the waves get stronger, there's not as much give, and there's certainly more judgment from the ranks. Sometimes it may feel as if you are sailing alone. You may even be told to stop sailing, as I was on more than one occasion. The good news is you will not be alone forever, because no PIRATE is. You may even find yourself as a captain sooner than you planned with others looking to *you* for advice, direction, and inspiration—even your administrators. Then you will know it is time to build a bigger ship, and with all hands on deck, you will.

If you are ready to lead at your school—regardless of your title— try some of these ideas:

Squish the Squash

It took me a while to learn how to do this, but oh, the difference it made when I did. When those around you try to squash your excitement, kindly squish their squash right into the ground. When my colleague told me to keep quiet during that staff meeting, I was a new teacher in the district and did not want to cause any trouble. If I could go back in time, I would have raised my hand and voiced my excitement for professional learning communities. Our passion should never be stifled, so be bold! Squish the squash, and your opportunities to lead will grow. Those who enjoy your excitement will jump on board, and eventually, even some of those who are hesitant will come around.

Start with Students

Leading a crew of students will open the doors of your classroom (or school) and ooze PIRATE learning into the hallways, school events, and social media. Yes, there will be those who do not understand your methods and choose to not take your lead, but if you do not take a chance with students and offer your leadership together, you will for sure be depriving teachers, students, and administrators who would follow your lead if they were only given the chance.

Get Students Leading PD

As it is often hard to sell ideas to colleagues and administrators, have students do it instead. It is impossible to argue with what kids are selling because everything they share is evidence that it works. Just a few years ago, I had four students lead two sessions on BrainPOP's newest features. There was not a teacher or administrator in the room disengaged, and every attendee advanced their use of BrainPOP soon after.

Take the Class out of the Room

The power in students teaching each other is invaluable. A few years ago, our class began offering teaching services to other classes. They had learned how to use BrainPOP. Several classes signed up for us to come in and lead students on a new BrainPOP adventure. Every one of my students became a personal teacher. Teachers were able to learn from my students and theirs.

Just this past year, second- and third-grade classes worked on mastering particular apps so that they could teach others how to use them. We split the classes up. Students were able to venture outside of their own rooms and teach one another.

Summary

PIRATE does not exist without *transformation*. It is not easy, but then again, it is not supposed to be. We can lead ourselves and work tirelessly to lead our students. Yet taking the culture of a school on a ride requires leading beyond the classroom and into hallways near and far. If you are an administrator who is already in the position to lead a building, please never take for granted the opportunity to make a difference in the lives of those you serve. Our titles alone do not make us effective. It is how we lead beyond them and dive into uncharted waters that will inspire a school to follow us and empower others to lead.

Leadership Treasure Hunt
(Find This)

Look for someone in your building who is not afraid to lead those around them, who does not keep his or her impact behind closed doors. Reach out to this person. Have a conversation. Soak up as much knowledge as you can and become inspired to make your mark on your own leadership journey.

Navigating the Seas
(Think about This)

Do you consider yourself a PIRATE? Which letter do you identify with the most? How does this letter guide you in your teaching? In your leading?

Charting the Course
(Take Action)

Wherever you are on your PIRATE journey, determine your next step. Whether it is taking calculated risks, inspiring the teacher next door, spreading hooks around your building, or focusing on relationships with your students. Whatever it is, go for it.

Share your thoughts and ideas!
#LeadLAP

LOOKING INWARD TO MOVE AHEAD

Becoming a PIRATE leader is a journey. We encourage you to use your passions to help you chart your course and to help you recalculate when you get off course.

—Shelley Burgess and Beth Houf, *Lead Like a PIRATE*

Another leadership component that sets PIRATE leaders apart is our role in helping others identify and tap into their passions.

—Shelley Burgess and Beth Houf, *Lead Like a PIRATE*

I can't believe that you won't be teaching at Hopkins next year, but you have accomplished something so great that you deserve to share it with the rest of the world!! You must be taking a huge step out of your comfort zone and using courage the whole way!!

—Maura

If any group of kids was going to keep me in the classroom, it was Crew 202. If any group of kids was going to push me out of the classroom, it was Crew 202. When your kids become leaders, they not only inspire and empower each other, they do the same for you. I had always had a passion for digital learning, so I decided to jump into being a technology integration specialist the next school year. I did not quite know what I was doing, but I made it my mission to figure it out. It was far from perfect, and then it was amazing.

The role of a technology integration specialist is often misunderstood—it is never really about the technology; it is about leveraging impact. I know and care way more about pedagogy than I do about technical support. The only reason I took on this role is because when kids are excited, I am all-in. I could see the power technology gave my students to connect with one another and an authentic audience, how it empowered them to create and allowed them to run with their own learning. I wanted to bring this same kind of enthusiasm for twenty-first-century learning that my students had experienced to as many learners as I possibly could. It had changed them. It had changed me. It was almost a crime not to share.

My first year as the K–3 technology integration coordinator for our district was the year of many mistakes. I felt as if I were rolling snowballs way too quickly and uphill. I was thinking like a classroom teacher with twenty-four bright-eyed and bushy-tailed students in front of me. But that approach did not work the same way with the hundred-plus teachers and administrators I was trying to encourage and inform. It is not that I did not go to my principals and the technology director and even superintendent first with my ideas for igniting the learning techniques that worked in my PIRATE classroom. I even took all of the necessary steps to involve both schools in a video with more than a thousand students and educators from our district. Putting logistics and enthusiasm first made me feel like I was doing the right thing, but I had missed something important: true connection. We can shout from the rooftops, but that is too far away to know if anyone is listening.

> Putting logistics and enthusiasm first made me feel like I was doing the right thing, but I had missed something important: true connection.

I am pretty extroverted, have a good sense for social situations, and usually use intuition to read a person during a conversation and often before one starts. Getting to know my students was always priority, and I immensely enjoyed hanging out with my colleagues. But I had never truly led them. So although I was flying high connecting with students and getting them excited about amazing learning experiences that I was modifying for each grade level, I did not reach every adult. I even pushed some away by bombarding their inbox. Many jumped on board, but for months, I shoved my passion on colleagues and administrators without investing nearly enough time in learning about theirs.

As much as I still adore the learning strategies we used in my classroom and what they did for my students, it was not until I had a few difficult meetings that I realized I needed to dig deep and reflect on my approach. When I was able to do this, ironically, I was able to use my own superpower of courage to its fullest ability. In the classroom, I had passed the mic to students, and I was still encouraging hundreds to lead. But in this new role, I was kind of a mic hog when it came to my colleagues. Realizing that, I gave my own passion a back seat to another letter in PIRATE I knew needed to take the wheel: rapport. I still was not quite sure how I would lead and definitely did not know how to get colleagues leading each other, but what I did know is that I was a good person with good intentions, and this brought me hope that people would trust me.

In the months that followed, I used the following approaches to help build rapport:

Show Up

No matter for what, and especially when you only have a minute, when a teacher, administrator, (or most importantly, a student) needs you, show up. When I made the conscious effort to show up face to face, at a moment's notice, my colleagues and I talked about and solved issues that were important to them. If time ran out, they knew I would come back, and I did. This helped to establish a deeper sense of trust, and relationships blossomed.

Put People First

When I helped colleagues with ideas and initiatives that were important to them, I walked away happy, and even better, so did they. I realized then that connecting with my peers served my true passion: people. My love for helping people was what made me the teacher I was, and it contributed to my becoming a better leader.

Tell Your People the Plan

During my second year as a technology integration specialist, I begged for two minutes in a staff meeting to explain my plan. It was the first time I was not demonstrating how to use Google for the evaluation system. These were *my* two minutes. I unwrinkled a tiny piece of paper with notes, spoke way too quickly, missed many with the details of new initiatives I was going to launch, but I made sure to make this message clear: *I am connecting with students, but I want to connect more with all of you. I want to reach you.* That was my new mission. I would hand the mic back, slow down, and listen, and I did just that. Whoever your audience is, tell them your plan loud and clear. It might just be the spark for stronger relationships.

Ask "How am I Doing?"

Face-to-face meetings are ideal, but if time does not allow for this, get creative. Last year, I started sending out a survey to staff called, "How Am I Doing?" Results have remained positive because I chose to put relationships first. Rapport matters.

Summary

Rapport is essential. We must push ourselves to be aware of what is happening around us, ask and analyze, and transform when necessary. If you feel even an inkling of doubt that your approach is not working, regardless of your title and regardless of who your audience is, take a breath and pause. Although you might not be the cause for the loss of connection, reflection and investigation are always a good tactic. Taking a breath and pausing will force you to slow down and ask why. Figuring out the answers will push you toward finding solutions to help you connect with others—and *that* is worth every second if you desire to be an effective leader.

Leadership Treasure Hunt
(Find This)

Whether with students, colleagues, or administrators, it is easy to be blinded by our own initiatives and what a great job we *think* we are doing. The hardest and even most valuable action you can take as a leader is to look around your classroom or school and identify those with whom you do not have a strong connection—yet.

 ## Navigating the Seas
(Think about This)

Has rapport ever taken a back seat in your initiative? What did you do? How did you reflect and change or if you are having an eye-opening moment right now, what will you do to reflect and change?

 ## Charting the Course
(Take Action)

If you are not sure where the people you work with stand on their relationship with you, be courageous and ask them!

Share your thoughts and ideas!
#LeadLAP

FINDING YOUR LEADERSHIP SUPERPOWER

Leading your crew to new exciting
places takes courage.

–Shelley Burgess and Beth Houf, *Lead Like a PIRATE*

Mark Twain defines courage as "resistance to fear,
mastery of fear, not absence of fear."

– Chip Heath and Dan Heath, *The Power of Moments*

I learned from my students that holding on to the dream of what we knew we could become might be the most important thing we can do for ourselves and others—even when the work it took to achieve that dream felt scary or meant that we would face judgment. Standing up for our dreams is what sets us apart as leaders.

Although I knew strengthening relationships would be key to my success as a leader, I also knew that sitting down with colleagues would not quite be enough. I knew I was wired for more. If I did not tap into my superpower of courage and carry it in my pocket as I had promised my students I would, I would be limiting myself as a leader. To find your leadership superpower, it takes great effort and reflection. To use it takes *chutzpah*.

> To find your leadership superpower, it takes great effort and reflection. To use it takes *chutzpah*.

Up until the year 2012, I worked with a coteacher. Then, for the first time ever, I was on my own as a teacher, and I was scared. (Ironically, 2012 also ignited a personal journey of presenting at conferences, which was a blast for me.) When Colleen Worrell, the high school technology integration coordinator and a parent of one of my students at the time, noticed at a curriculum night that I might just have something to offer other educators, she prompted me to share more.

Today, Colleen is a good friend and #leadlapmass colauncher. She is also the reason I switched roles! She saw something in me beyond what I had been able to see in myself and convinced me to put myself out there. Over the next several years, through leading sessions on blended learning, strengths- and passion-based approaches, and just about anything PIRATE, I began to realize that maybe Colleen was onto something. I could, in fact, engage teachers, not just students and parents, in meaningful ways. But I was not completely convinced, until a wedding one night on the other side of the country, that my approach to connecting with an audience was unique.

My closest friend from college was married a few years ago, and she put it out there that anyone who wanted to say something at the reception could. I said *yes* immediately. Suddenly, it was go time, and similarly to the moment of announcing piracy, my leg was shaking. I had courage in my pocket, tapped into my inner superhero, and stayed faithful to my PIRATE roots, never backing down from any risk worth taking. Within a second of my arrival on the dance floor, I managed to make everyone nervous. No script in hand like the others who came before me, I spoke from the heart, and it worked. I had the crowd laughing, and afterward, so many people I had not met before that night came up to me and commented on my speech. The stakes that night had been as high as any I would ever give as it was captured in a video as part of one of the most cherished nights this special couple would ever have.

I realized that night, finally, that I had the ability to get up in front of a crowd and connect a room full of strangers and friends. My two minutes in the spotlight at that one morning staff meeting hardly made me a leader, but over time, I leaned in to my courage, honed my skills, and developed my superpower of connecting with people. That is how I learned to leave an impact that lasts.

If you are wondering what your leadership superpower is, here are a few ideas to help you find it, so you can lead right where you are:

Say *Yes!*

Saying *yes* is a goal of mine not only as a PIRATE educator but also as a PIRATE *human*. When you commit to taking risks you would normally say no to, everything changes. Saying yes boosts your confidence, which is essential if you want to discover the qualities that make you the leader you are—and the leader you can become.

Honor the PIRATE Moments Outside of School

It is amazing how connected our personal and educational lives truly are. We must honor the risks we are willing to take outside of school and learn the importance of their potential in our educational lives. Pay close attention to the next piratey thing you do in your personal life. Brainstorm ways you can bring the experience into school to make an even greater impact.

Be Relentless About Being Yourself

Every year, I watch teachers endure parent nights and open houses as if they cannot wait until the event is over! These occasions are an opportune time to show everyone who you are. It is also the perfect time to discover and sharpen the qualities that make you stand out— those traits that make people want to follow you. You never know which parents in the crowd or which administrators walking through the halls will be paying close attention.

You do not have to be loud or boisterous to show people the real you; in fact, some of the most amazing PIRATE leaders I have met are quiet leaders. The nonnegotiable point is that you must be true to *yourself*.

Uncover and Use Your Hidden Superpowers

When you confidently use one of your superpowers, others start to surface. Through speaking and connecting, I discovered that creativity was one of my superpowers. Colleen helped me discover my superpower for speaking simply by noticing it and encouraging me to share more. What traits and skills do people compliment you on? What seems to come naturally to you that others struggle with? Those abilities or characteristics may well be superpowers that you have not paid attention to (yet) because they seem "normal" or easy for you. Tap into them!

Reflect!

Ask yourself, "What is it like to be in my classroom?" and "What do parents learn from being in my classroom?" Your answers can help you discover your unique leadership skills. The goal, no matter who's watching, is to bring your best self to the experiences you are creating. When people leave your room (Or school!), be it your students or parents who are attending open-house events, they should walk away knowing your superpowers—and so should you!

Summary

We cannot ignore the superpowers that make us unique—the traits that make us stand out as leaders. Relationships will always be at the heart of what I do and, more importantly, why I do it. For me, that means show up whenever and wherever I am needed. It also means being unafraid to use the mic *and* being willing to pass it to others so I can listen to what they have to say too.

Dig deep and determine your greatest superpower and then have the courage to use it to contribute to your effective leadership. When you unleash your greatest strengths, you will inspire followers, and your potential for leading will become limitless.

Leadership Treasure Hunt
(Find This)

Make it your mission to look for rock-star moments—
those that happen to you, and even those that happen to
others—inside of school and out. Pay attention to what you
learn about yourself and your peers from those moments.

Navigating the Seas
(Think about This)

What are your strengths? How are you using them in
your role to lead students and/or staff? What is the
one strength (or superpower) you simply must use as a
leader so you don't cheat yourself and others?

Charting the Course
(Take Action)

Discover your leadership superpower and conquer your
fear of using it. If you have already mastered one, tap into
the next! Make it your mission to bring your strengths to
life. When in doubt, grab some *chutzpah*. It is free.

Share your thoughts and ideas!
#LeadLAP

SEEING YOUR SCHOOL THROUGH A PROBLEM SOLVING LENS

Good questions inform; great questions transform.

—Shelley Burgess and Beth Houf, *Lead Like a PIRATE*

Nevertheless, think about your constraints for a moment—not as barriers to your ability to innovate, but instead as a puzzle that holds the opportunity for creativity and great work.

—David Sturt, an executive vice president at O.C. Tanner

My crew of SuperPIRATE students had shown me the power of asking questions. When I shifted into the role of technology integration coordinator, I had so many questions starting with *When and how could I reach teachers most effectively? What was I doing that wasn't working? How would I ever break the barrier of "there's just no time"?*

To find insights on those questions and others, I reached out to an expert in my field who also happens to be a friend, Casey Echelmeier, instructional technology specialist for Mexico Public Schools in Missouri. I took notes as she told me about the initiatives she had been able to ignite in her district. When we signed off, I was filled with gratitude, inspiration, hope, and ideas.

Soon after my conversation with Casey, my administrator at the second- and third-grade building gave me *fifteen whole minutes* to talk to my school's staff. The problem was that those fifteen minutes would be at 7:45 A.M. the morning after Super Bowl 2017. It was the worst possible time to reach staff and quite possibly the best.

I am in Massachusetts, which means the interest in the game was intensely high. I, of course, believed with all of my heart that the Patriots would win, so I included a victory GIF on the first slide of my presentation. (Just in case, I had a second opening slide ready in the event that the Patriots lost.) It may seem insignificant, but that personal touch was one of the most important things I could have done to connect with my colleagues that morning. The Patriots won and, with the help of lots of coffee that morning (thanks to our administrators), energy and positivity filled the air, despite the fact that we had all stayed up late to celebrate.

My fifteen-minute session consisted of seventeen slides, each one oozing with empowerment and encouragement. I courageously pushed teachers to think about the twenty-first century classroom, where they were, and where they could be. I shared inspiring quotes and videos by rock-star educators and talked about the innovation happening within the walls of our school. And when I showed them what students had to say about the kind of classroom they ache for, I watched as the realization hit home in my colleagues' hearts that perhaps it was time to think differently about learning.

To support my colleagues in launching their twenty-first century adventures, I provided a customizable action plan. It was just fifteen minutes, but I was able to empower those around me, which is just what I had set out to do. In that short time, the teachers and administrators I served began to see me as someone who was a thoughtful and confident individual, and most importantly, who was invested in them and their students. I would like to think they even began to see me as a leader. Teachers from every pocket of the building started taking new risks—from trying a few technology tools to blending lessons and units. The best part of this shift was that colleagues began to lead each other.

Teachers from every pocket of the building started taking new risks—from trying a few technology tools to blending lessons and units.

Here are a few ideas to help you become a problem solver and make the impact you were meant to make.

Ask for Help Even When It Hurts

We are in the profession of leading students, so it is hard to let go of the idea that we have to be perfect. But *perfect* is unrealistic, and it is not good for kids; it is incredibly boring! I reached out to Casey because I knew I needed help. I knew my *why*, but I needed guidance on *how* to initiate and implement the kind of changes I wanted to see in our school. Admittedly I was a bit jealous when Casey first shared with me about the successes she had experienced in her district (It even hurt a little because I felt as if I had been failing!). Even though it hurt my pride a bit to ask for help, our conversation was exactly what I needed.

Meet Your People Exactly Where They Are

If you have any shot of showing colleagues, administrators, and students where they can be, you must first meet them where they are. I knew that the staff I would be talking to on the morning after the Super Bowl would be exhausted after a late night of celebrating. Engaging them with something they cared about was the key to my success that day. And it worked. Teachers even asked me to share the GIF I had shared, so they could project it in their classrooms when their students walked in later that morning.

Include the Voice of Students

The GIF was fun, but the most powerful piece of information I shared during that meeting was a word cloud showing how students felt about learning with technology. Before I showed the image, I asked the staff to complete the same survey (through Answer Garden). When we compared the results, the difference was stark. Students focused on words like *fun, empowerment,* and *teamwork.* Teachers focused on the actual devices and technology. Including student voices gave the teachers a new and important perspective. Whenever you are seeking to lead change, include the voices of students in the discussion. After all, students are the reason we show up every single day. Their voices are too often missed; you can be the one to make sure they are heard.

Do Not Just Talk a Good Game, Up It

Believe you can do more, reach more, and make it happen. I was able to quickly provide more meaningful tech tips, create how-to videos, and offer real-life "Delicious Demos" with treats and coffee on several mornings throughout the year. Although I was in a computer lab with a set schedule, I used every available second to talk and work with teachers, administrators, and students. So do not just talk about it. Go out there and up your game by creating solutions for those you serve and for yourself!

Summary

Making yourself vulnerable to the ideas of others can inspire hope, and that hope can become a commitment to action. When you choose to listen first and provide relevant solutions and ideas, you can help your colleagues, administrators, and students unleash their initiatives and passions.

Leadership Treasure Hunt
(Find This)

Reflect for a moment on problems you are seeing either in your role, classroom, or building. Make a conscious effort to pay attention to where a solution is needed.

Navigating the Seas
(Think about This)

When is the last time you found yourself looking for solutions? To whom did you reach out for help or input? What was your action plan and what happened as a result of implementation?

Charting the Course
(Take Action)

Make it a priority to reach out to experts in your field, read books, and listen to podcasts. Do whatever it takes to stay current and motivated. Create an action plan that makes sense to you, your students and/or staff, and launch it. The worst that can happen is that it will fail. If/when that happens, get creative, and try something else. That is, after all, what problem solvers do.

Share your thoughts and ideas!
#LeadLAP

Putting Passion into Practice with Staff!

Painting a picture through stories that capture people's hearts is much more effective at initiating change than sharing pages and pages of data charts.

—Shelley Burgess and Beth Houf, Lead Like a PIRATE

If we are going to crush apathy in our schools and create learning that's irresistible, it won't happen by doubling down our efforts to reach proficiency. We have to start by developing environments where students can rekindle what it means to be a passionate learner.

After all, they came to us this way, right?

—David Geurin

O n the last day of school in the second year of my new role, an assembly of five hundred students and staff laughed along as we watched principals, students, teachers, and parents playing games and having fun during our school's first-ever cardboard arcade. When the video was over, our principal said, "This is what happens when people share their passion and put their heads together." (You can watch it here: bit.ly/Cardboardarcade.)

We want our students to run to get *into* school—and we need that same kind of excitement for each day. For that to happen, learning has to matter. It has to be engaging and meaningful to everyone. In my own classroom and my current position, I would become convinced that the best way to make learning something that kids and teachers are excited about is to use a hands-on, learner-led approach. To that end, we implemented Genius Hour, designed a cardboard arcade, and had hosted several Student Edcamps. All of those initiatives demonstrated to our school community that passion and innovation matter—a lot.

As LaVonna Roth pointed out during a Skype session with the first third-grade class to take on Genius Hour, students who participated in this learning experience did not just create projects; they developed solutions. Beyond becoming aware of and even spreading the word about endangered animals, a hurting environment, and food-and-water shortages, these passion-based projects put students in the role of innovators. They become determined to solve problems that are meaningful to them.

When we give students a say in what they want to explore and study, learning becomes important and valuable in a way that worksheets can never be. And the learning does not stop when the school bell rings. I have seen students rush home to build prototypes or to FaceTime their partners to plan next steps. The elementary students who built the arcade blew their parents, teachers, administrators (and

> When we give students a say in what they want to explore and study, learning becomes important and valuable in a way that worksheets can never be.

peers) away with the level of devotion they gave their learning as well as level of expertise they were able to display.

The same thing happens to us as educators when we discover our passions and pursue and create solutions.

Here are a few ideas to help you open doors, knock them down, and put passion into practice.

Check out our school's first-ever Genius Hour: bit.ly/3rdgradegeniushour

Create the Bait

I created a S'more flyer representing a menu of digital tools as well as twenty-first century approaches when I began my technology role. Just as I would do with students, I threw out some unique deep-dive ideas, seeing who would eat them up and make them their own. This was important because many teachers had not taken a dive into learning that challenged them to develop ideas, create, and solve problems right alongside their students. Yet many were hungry for it. A few teachers who were willing to explore their own passion of teaching with relevancy and giving kids opportunities to make a difference took the "Genius Hour" bait. From there, a conversation around passion (and purpose) based learning was born. So do not be afraid, regardless of your audience, to create the bait. Nurture those who take the first bite. Chances are, you will put your heads together and do amazing things. Teachers who are willing to reveal their passion, from my experience, have never regretted the decision of diving further in.

Inspire with Stories of Others

Many times we forget that we do not have to be completely original. Everything I did in the classroom with students was in some way inspired from something or someone else. The truth is that what we bring to our schools and classrooms will always be different because we are all different. Share your stories and what you have learned as often as possible. Take inspiration from the ideas you hear from others and make them your own. When kids see kids doing something amazing, their first human reaction is to ask, "Can we do that?" I believe this reaction also lives in the heart of every educator. Yet we hear over and over that there is simply no time or that line we know too well that is hard for me to even put on paper: "There's no way *my* class can handle that." So when three teachers came to me because they realized that students sharing their own passions was, in fact, an educational passion of theirs, we made time for Edcamp, we tweaked the structure, we learned from my experiences and those of others, and my colleagues were beside themselves with the outcome. Bring your stories and share them. If you do not, more teachers who are aching to put their passion into practice but are unsure how to do so may go on teaching from a place of being stuck rather than a place of freedom.

Bring your stories and share them.

Call on Those Who Have Been There

Invite former students in to share their stories face to face. Videos are great, and over the past two years, I have used many starring my former students to empower a new crew of young learners. Yet there is nothing like having a panel to share individual experiences face to face. Do not stop there. Hire them as change-making ambassadors. My students (now eighth graders!) came in to help third graders during Genius Hour as sixth and seventh graders. Their support was beyond impactful. There is immense power in kids empowering kids, and I believe there always will be. What the mentoring relationship also accomplished was reaching a strength in both myself and my Genius Hour colleague: connecting with students. Being able to bring students back not only brought out our strength but showed all students involved how much respect we have for their generation. It showed them what immense power we believe they have in leading each other, which is, of course, the greatest passion my colleague and I share.

Capture Like Crazy

You do not have to be a professional photographer or videographer. In fact, apps like Quik do most of the work! Just make sure you are in the moment, immersed with capturing every second of learning, joy, and empowerment. If you want support, ask someone in a role like mine or even a parent! I have done both! The point is, the power in others learning from our stories, especially when expressed with pictures, videos, and music, is invaluable when it comes to inspiring others. We also take the leap into being the people doing the inspiring. There is nothing like students inspiring students in the same building. Everyone wants in. As I began to take pictures and create videos myself, colleagues became more inspired to capture their own moments with students. Not only that, but they were motivated to create learning that would be worth capturing!

Have an Open-Door Policy

In an IMMOOC episode (Innovator's Mindset MOOC, which is a massive open online course based on the book *The Innovator's Mindset* by George Couros) with John Spencer and Angela Watson, Katie Martin explained that opening classroom doors so teachers can see what's really happening as one of her favorite strategies to move from pockets of innovation to school wide change. There's a much greater chance to inspire our colleagues if we allow them to see the whole picture. Letting others see "behind the scenes" will give them the confidence to say, "We can do this!" It also gives us a window into each other's passions.

Hype Up Sharing with a School/District Hashtag

In *Lead Like a PIRATE*, Shelley and Beth discuss the importance of sharing your school story, and Beth has created a platform for sharing through #fmsteach, which I highly recommend checking out! Creating a school hashtag is a blast. Pushing people to use it may take some time, but the moment you see even two colleagues sharing what's happening in their classroom, it is worth the effort! Typically teachers who tweeted to our hashtag were thrilled to share something they truly enjoyed with their students. This mattered as it strengthened our relationships and started us talking about our work as educators and how we could put our heads together to impact our students.

Summary

Whether they chose to bring Genius Hour, Student Edcamp, or building a cardboard arcade to students, those third-grade teachers in our school felt a call to action. They embraced cutting-edge, student-led approaches to learning, and in doing so, found renewed energy for themselves. Peers (both of the students and the teachers) who witnessed the student-owned learning in action were inspired to try it themselves. By simply sharing what they were doing, these students and teachers led others to take risks.

Regardless of our titles, we must get to know our colleagues, put our heads together, listen to one another's passions, and act. What is possible in the classroom is what you make time for, and there's no wasted time when students (and teachers) are learning. And when you share what you are doing, your impact will be felt throughout the school—and beyond!

Leadership Treasure Hunt
(Find This)

Who is hungry to dive deep? Is it your students?
Your colleagues? Your administrators? Make it a
mission to discover who is ready and start with
them. The ripple effect will amaze you.

Navigating the Seas
(Think about This)

What are you doing to help your colleagues and
administrators launch a deep-dive adventure full of
passionate learning? For students? For staff? How
might you launch a new one of your own?

Charting the Course
(Take Action)

Whether it is a lesson, unit, or yearlong mission, dive deep
into the water with your students, colleagues, administrators, or all three. The depth of learning will only grow for
everyone involved, and what you discover will most likely
be something you just cannot see from the surface.

Share your thoughts and ideas!
#LeadLAP

SHIFTING THE STAFF MEETING MINDSET

So don't be afraid to put yourself out there.
Share who you are, what you're passionate
about, and how it motivates you to lead.

—Shelley Burgess and Beth Houf, *Lead Like a PIRATE*

Finding time to share great ideas with our district's teachers and administrators is always a challenge–but it never hurts to ask, particularly when you have an idea that can help others reach *their* goals. I happened to know that the K–1 campus I worked with was looking for ways to both reduce paper use and increase technology application with its young students. Bingo! That was my angle. I sent an email to the principal of our K–1 building and addressed her stated need to cut paper cost. And of course, I promised to empower her teachers to try something new.

At first, she agreed to give me twenty minutes during a staff meeting. After we went through what the meeting *could* look like if we structured it thoughtfully, she ended up giving me an hour and a half—and I was determined to use every second. I went in with a plan and then made it happen. Here is how things went down:

3:30

I invited all staff members and administrators to join Quizlet Live to play what turned out to be one competitive game. The terms were based on the twenty-first-century learning tools and approaches we explored during the meeting. Curiosity, intensity, and pure determination to win spread across the room as the teams worked together.

We listened intently when the winning team shared strategies that contributed to their success, which I highly recommend trying with students. I also encouraged teams that disagreed with any definitions to let me know as I believe arguing in the classroom can be healthy!

3:50ish

We explored the benefits of the Quizlet game. How did this activity help in terms of previewing content? How did it help us tap into our soft skills? How could we potentially use it in the classroom?

During this time, I shared my passion for twenty-first-century teaching and learning and made sure to compliment my colleagues on the amazing work they were doing every day. We also took time to reflect on ways we could each shift our mindset to do an even better job meeting our kids where they are. Since it is easy to feel overwhelmed by the vast amount of digital tools available, I told teachers the focus should not be on the technology itself but rather how to use it as an avenue to empowerment. And as we continued, I asked my colleagues and administrators to think about the following questions:

- What is one thing you can do to get you and your students running to school every day?
- What is one digital tool you are already using that you could expand your practice with?
- What is one digital tool could you explore in order to bring student-centered learning to the next level?
- How would you develop your technology radar?
- How could you transform your classroom into an environment where students own their learning?

4:00ish

Five teachers courageously shared a risk they have taken in the classroom. They provided us with the process, the challenges, and the undeniable positive results. Passion-based learning, STEAM, innovation, Kahoot, Seesaw, BrainPOP Jr., and Quizlet were all hot topics. Through sharing real stories and revealing engaging videos, the crowd was hooked. This was my favorite part of the meeting, and it was part of the plan. I contacted each teacher before the meeting and empowered them to lead. Their input was invaluable as it showed the results of what I was encouraging staff to try.

4:20ish

For thirty magical minutes, teachers and administrators chose a topic to explore. Most explored an idea that had just been presented. A few others, however, chose a completely new topic. Throughout the room, ideas sparked discussions. Teachers created accounts on new apps they wanted to try. Some took tours of passion-based centers while others developed playful assessments.

By 4:50, the enthusiasm for learning was still going strong. Normally, right before 5:00, keys start to jingle, and people put on their coats. It is human nature to be exhausted after a long day of work . . . or is it?

4:50ish

It took me three tries to get everyone's attention, and to be completely honest, I did not want to. It was important, however, that my colleagues not only acknowledged their accomplishment for the afternoon but celebrated it. In addition, I wanted them to make a commitment to it. Teachers joined a Padlet I had created, so they could share what they would put into action.

5:00ish

We walked out of the building with new energy. I was given the chance to share who *I* am because I asked and because I created a structure that aimed for success. I grabbed an opportunity to inspire my peers and, most importantly, push them to inspire each other.

In just one staff meeting, teachers led, shared, responded to each other with enthusiasm, and demonstrated immense trust and support. Even after the meeting, they continued to expand their ideas, explore new ones, and took risks to try something new with a focus on their passions.

Staff meetings are a built-in time for professional development. Whether you have twenty minutes or ninety, here are a few ideas that may help you craft opportunities to transform the traditional staff meeting in your building and maybe even beyond!

> Even after the meeting, they continued to expand their ideas, explore new ones, and took risks to try something new with a focus on their passions.

Ask for Time!

If you have an idea that would benefit your school, ask for time at your next meeting to share. Go in with a plan, lay it all out, and make sure you are meeting the needs of your administrators and staff. If you have a clear map for running a whole staff meeting, you may discover that your administrators are thrilled at the prospect of a little less prep work for them!

Stick to the Staff Meeting Plan

If you have a shot at ever leading a staff meeting again, stick to the plan you shared with your administrator. Realize that you are not just trying to run a staff meeting; you are trying to prove that your unconventional way of leading it is worth the hour—and every minute after when folks actually use what they have learned. You are also trying to show your leaders something about *you*. For me, the goal was to show my administrators that although my ideas may seem "out there," my message and organization, when it comes to teachers' learning, are always crystal clear.

Embrace the "Last Staff Meeting Ever" Mindset

Go into your meeting like it is the *last staff meeting ever*! Make it your goal to see your colleagues so invested in their learning that they actually forget about the clock. Identify what your colleagues are doing when they have reached their highest level of engagement and become relentless about encouraging this kind of learning again. If you are in a building where your colleagues have never ignored the clock, it is certainly time. Go out there and rock their world.

Do Some Research and Present Your Findings

I have found *Learner-Centered Innovation* by Katie Martin, *The Four O'Clock Faculty* by Rich Czyz, and *Lead Like a PIRATE* by Shelley Burgess and Beth Houf to be invaluable tools regarding sharing ideas for professional growth. I have pulled ideas directly from these books and others, as well as podcasts and conferences to share with teachers and administrators. (I have even given these books as gifts to my administrators!) Learn and share everything you can.

Summary

The ideas, lessons, approaches, and tools that get us running into school are the gems that empower us and empower our students. Creating opportunities for staff to share these gems is certainly essential to leadership and a whole lot of fun.

In *Learner-Centered Innovation*, Katie Martin stresses the need for educators to become learners in order to have the greatest impact on students. During that unconventional staff meeting two years ago, teachers and administrators had opportunities to learn differently, and they left with the opportunity to teach differently. It may seem risky to ask for time to share during a staff meeting, but schools need educators who are willing to take those risks! Craft a structure that meets staff and administrators where they are but also encourages progress.

Leadership Treasure Hunt
(Find This)

Search for opportunities where you can offer something that meets a need in your school. You will never know how welcomed your idea will be unless you present it. Make sure you do so in a timely manner before the issue is forgotten!

Navigating the Seas
(Think about This)

How often do you ask your administrators for time at a staff meeting? If this is something you never do, what is stopping you? If you are an administrator, what is your priority during your staff meetings? How often do you allow teachers time to share who they are and what gets them running into school? If this is not a part of your practice, what is stopping you from making it happen?

Charting the Course
(Take Action)

Whether it is a ninety-minute staff meeting or five minutes at the beginning, whether it is through social media or face to face, whether you start with one individual or many, show your staff members who you are and why you run to school. When you are ready, schedule a conversation with your administrator, ask for time with staff, and do not forget to bring their WHY with you. Just make sure to bring yours too. There is nothing like teachers learning from teachers. If the answer is no, get creative. It might be time to go rogue.

Share your thoughts and ideas!
#LeadLAP

DEFINING AND CRAFTING YOUR ROLE

Does your supervisor know your passions and what you stand for in education?

—Shelley Burgess and Beth Houf, *Lead Like a PIRATE*

'WHY do you do what you do?' is actually quite simple and efficient to discover. It's the discipline to never veer from your cause, to hold yourself accountable to HOW you do things; that's the hardest part.

—Simon Sinek, *Start With Why*

As a classroom teacher, I knew my WHY–the reason I ran to school every single day. I wanted to empower my students and push them to empower each other. And then I expanded that WHY to empowering teachers to bring student-owned learning to the classroom. When I started sharing my why—and the WHATS and HOWS—things began to change for me and for the teachers I served. I watched some find new freedom to create their own WHY and act on it. But the exact roads to get from their WHY to the actions and strategies still seemed fuzzy—for me and for the people I wanted to reach and empower. I knew there had to be a better tactic than begging for a few minutes here and there in staff meetings.

I knew what I had to do, and it required an uncomfortable conversation. I scheduled a fifteen-minute meeting with the principal of the second- and third-grade building where I spent a lot of my time—and where I saw opportunities for improvement in twenty-first-century learning. I went in with a plan to say one thing: "I feel underused." Simple but heavy. Once again, things began to change for me—and for the school—simply because I spoke up. I was transparent about the fact that I wanted to do more. I saw a mountain ahead of me and, although the foundation was solid, I was ready for a hike.

The principal asked me to break down all the ways I desired to be used. So I did, and I went big. I reflected on my role and what it could be. I considered all that had happened in the previous two years and what I wanted to change. I also knew that snagging more time to reach colleagues during staff meetings would be a challenge, so I provided alternate routes for greatest impact.

My schedule confined me to a computer lab with technology classes. It allowed very little time for me to be in the classroom and almost never allowed me to attend professional learning community (PLC) meetings. The learning I was able to offer from my lab was bound to certain devices, and transferring ideas, skills, and lessons into the classroom was challenging. Students knew my WHY for them was discovering what makes them awesome and using purposeful technology to leverage their learning experiences, but my HOWS were not meeting my vision for students or their teachers. I needed to fight for full-time integration.

Defining and crafting a role that would allow me to make the most impact helped me push past the boundaries of preconceived limitations. I think the same thing can happen for you! Here are a few ideas that will help you define what you do and create a vision for those around you whether it is your administrators, colleagues, students, or families. Do not forget to go big!

Kindly Tell It Like It Is

Especially when attempting to change the culture in our buildings or even a whole district, we need to be honest with our leaders. If we do not feel that we are in a place where we are being used to our full capacity, we need to say something. Staying silent and keeping the status quo deprives our school communities of who we really are. Do not assume your leaders know what you are capable of or would like to try—tell them! Nothing will change without clear communication.

Spell It Out on Paper

When you clearly spell out your WHY, HOW, and WHAT on paper for your leaders, they will know what they are getting. Writing down your vision for your role provides an opportunity to reflect on what you do, why you do it, and where you think you might be headed. If you're struggling to define your desired role and your hopes for the future in relation to the impact you can make, ask yourself, "Why am I here?" Chances are, answering that question honestly may refuel you like never before.

Provide Evidence of Success

Regardless of your audience, support your idea with evidence. Defining my role pushed me to provide evidence of my success. The more stories of success you can include when sharing your vision with others, the more they will be inclined to listen and act. It is hard to argue against proof! If you are in the classroom, capture and share the work you do with your students and families. Sharing past successes is a great way to welcome new students into a legacy of awesome no one will want to miss.

Ask for Support

Let your audience (in my case administrators) know you need them. You do not—or should not—have all the answers. When you are trying to impact the culture of your school or classroom (even when defining *your* personal role), do not try to do it alone. Input from your community and leaders is essential to crafting a successful plan. Invite your administrators, colleagues, students, and families to be a part of a team!

Leave an Unconventional Thought to Ponder

When you craft your role, include your unique passion. Give your leader something unconventional to ponder. It is kind of like when an artist has a few hit songs on the radio, and then one day, you hear a song by the same artist that sounds different—but still has their unique sound. Even if you cannot sing along, you are willing to at least listen because you know the artist well enough to give the song a chance. It is these songs that are often not only the best but also show who the artist really is. Do not miss this chance to shine! Go for it.

Imagine the possibilities of modifying the below for your unique audience and, even better, asking them to create and share their own! Below is what I composed for my administrators:

- **My Main Goal**—to empower teachers and students with twenty-first-century teaching and learning.

- **My Role**—To me, empowering students (and teachers) is priority. I see twenty-first-century skills, approaches, and tools as a huge asset in addition to supporting all areas of curriculum. Blended learning plays a significant role within integrating technology, but I also see my role as integrating twenty-first-century approaches to support curriculum such as flipped learning, strength- and passion-based learning (Genius Hour, student-led Edcamps, etc.), student-led classrooms, project-based learning, design thinking, global awareness, innovative practices for professional development, and using social media to connect classrooms as well as teachers (within the district and beyond). I am looking for an opportunity to connect with teachers in more meaningful ways to serve as both a source of support and inspiration. I have seen risk-taking impact students greatly and would like to see this continue.

I went on to break down ideas and tactics for implementing changes that would allow me to use my strengths and expertise to empower students and teachers. I included strategies and time requests for professional development and offered suggestions for how they could be woven into the schools' existing schedules. The plan also showed how others could be called upon to share their ideas.

Sharing my vision and plan for what I could do to serve our teachers allowed my administrators to see new opportunities for learning and teaching. They read my hopes and dreams and listened during further conversations. Although I have not (yet) launched every single initiative on my list, change is happening, and progress is being made. The best thing that could have possibly happened did: my role became full-time integration. In the end, redefining my job description tion helped us all get what we wanted.

Summary

Never assume that your leaders, colleagues, students, or community know what you want to accomplish in your role. Take time to think about what you want to accomplish and then create a plan of action. Defining your role, even if you *do not* share it with anyone, can be a powerful way to get clarity on your WHYs, HOWs, and WHATs.

Leadership Treasure Hunt
(Find This)

Look for an opportunity to share the vision you have
for your role and determine who you most think
could benefit from knowing it. Is it your students?
Colleagues? School Community? All three?

Navigating the Seas
(Think about This)

When is the last time you ached to be used or do
more, to impact positive change in ways you knew
you were capable of? How did you communicate
this to those you felt needed to hear it?

Charting the Course
(Take Action)

Outline what you really want over the next school year or
even several months. Make sure your WHYs, HOWs, and
WHATs are clear. Share what you create with your administrators, colleagues, students, school community, and even
the world, but most importantly, share it with yourself. There
is nothing like seeing your own vision for the work you do
(and want to do) come to life on paper. Encourage your
colleagues and administrators and, yes, even your students to
do the same and ask them to share what they come up with.

Share your thoughts and ideas!
#LeadLAP

The Journey of a PIRATE Principal Who Leads with WHY

Jordan Hoffman, principal,
Johnson Elementary School, Natick, Massachusetts

During my first year as an elementary principal, I learned a lot about myself as a leader. I am relentless in my pursuit to make a difference. I am constantly seeking new ways to inspire, connect, and motivate the staff and students with whom I work. I am willing to be vulnerable, take risks, fail, and look ridiculous if need be. At first, I found this new role lonesome. I had always valued collaboration and then found myself in a position without close colleagues to share ideas and push my thinking.

After "lurking" on Twitter for quite some time, I began to make some professional connections. I was following #MomsasPrincipals, #PrincipalsinAction, and of course, #LeadLAP. In July, I boarded an Amtrak Train for Philadelphia to attend the National Principals Conference. I arrived in the city not really knowing anyone and completely out of my comfort zone. To my surprise, I spent three days surrounded by like-minded passionate leaders sharing struggles, successes, and ideas.

During an EdCamp facilitated by Joe Mazza, Jimmy Casas, and Joe Sanfelippo, I sat next to Beth Houf, where we swapped ideas about how to transform faculty meetings. When I shared that I was a principal in Natick, MA, she asked if I knew Nili Bartley. While Nili and I had connected on Twitter through the LeadLAP hashtag, we had not yet met in person. A month or two later, Nili reached out to ask if I wanted to present with her at my district's innovation-and-learning day. I agreed even though we still had not met. At the MassCue Conference in October, we did finally meet when she was presenting on Leading Like a PIRATE, and ironically, we presented a month later on the power of a professional learning network (PLN).

Aaron Hogan wrote in *Shattering the Perfect Teacher Myth*, "Twitter is not going to change your life. But the educators you meet there will." Because of the educators I have connected with through Twitter, I am continuously trying new things: BreakoutEDU for a staff meeting, celebrating students' birthdays by tweeting framed photos, presenting teachers with light-up hashtags and "worth it boxes" and sharing a video recording of a back-to-school read aloud for students in my bathrobe! The educators I have met on Twitter and through Voxer stretch my thinking and push me to be better every day.

> ## Twitter is not going to change your life. But the educators you meet there will.
> —Aaron Hogan, *Shattering the Perfect Teacher Myth*

Similarly to collaborative practices, Twitter breaks down the walls of our classrooms and schools allowing us to learn from one another. Robert John Meehan said, "The most valuable resource that all teachers have is each other. Without collaboration, our growth is limited to our own perspectives." I am a lifelong learner willing to be vulnerable, take risks, and step outside of my comfort zone in my pursuit to make a difference, and I am lucky to have a tribe to push me to be better every day.

PART THREE

TAKING THE LEADERSHIP PLUNGE

BELIEVING WE ARE MORE THAN OUR TITLES

A core value we hold true—one that helps shape the daily work we do as leaders—is the idea that we are all on the same team.

—Shelley Burgess and Beth Houf, *Lead Like a PIRATE*

The only way to make sense out of change is to plunge into it, move with it, and join the dance.

—Alan W. Watts

As leaders, I think we must invest every fiber of our belief and energy to help those we serve develop confidence and skills, so they can realize that leaders don't need a patch, badge, title, or nameplate to be considered a model teacher or a leader. It's the way we manage ourselves every day that allows us the privilege of leadership in whatever position we hold.

—Jimmy Casas, *Culturize*

I wanted to vomit. It was July 2017, and I was panicking. Beth Houf had just posted a Facebook link to an article I had written for the *Lead Like a PIRATE* blog. I felt honored to be featured on the blog, but for some reason, it had not occurred to me that she would post it on Facebook. So when I saw my blog post right there on Facebook, my stomach began to turn. *What if my colleagues read it? And even worse, what if my principal read it?*

I had been sharing my school life on Twitter for years, but in my mind, connections on that platform were with educators *outside of my school*. Facebook was personal—the connections there were people I knew in real life. If I had stopped to think about it, I would have acknowledged the fact that teaching *is* personal and social media is *social* media; it is natural for education connections on both of those platforms to be personal.

What in the world was I afraid of? *Misinterpretation.* I had worked so incredibly hard to put relationships first, and I worried they were suddenly at stake. I was afraid my teacher friends would think I might be leading *too* much. I was afraid of coming on too strong.

> ## I was afraid my teacher friends would think I might be leading too much.

I have learned, however, that we have to recognize our feelings of fear—even if they prevent us from digesting food—and we must, as Mark Twain suggests, master them. That is courage. That blog and subsequent Facebook post were an essential stop on my leadership journey. Beth knew that, and soon enough, I did too. I believed in what I had written. I was invested in the success of our school. And so

I reminded myself that sharing my expertise and insights with people I knew in real life was a good thing. I had not ruined anything; in fact, I had taken a very important step toward becoming the leader I wanted to be. Needless to say, there were no negative reactions. Just hearts.

Here are a few ideas to help you embrace the idea of plunging into leadership regardless of your title!

Have Your Bandage Ready

It is possible that someone will look at what you are doing, what you have written, what you are sharing, and not love it. This happens especially when you step outside of your job description. Negative comments can hurt, so have your bandage ready. Remind yourself that you believe in what you are doing for those you are serving. Know whom you can reach out to for support—the people in your life who know you, love you, and believe in you. Having a bandage plan ready and waiting might just actually give you more courage to share.

See Social Media as *Social* Media

It is completely okay to post an educational article on Facebook and post something personal on Twitter. Social media is social media. If you are afraid of what people in your building might think, you have two choices: never share or master your fear. I chose to master my fear, and I highly recommend it! This is what can happen when we are not afraid for our colleagues and administrators to see who we really are. You might even be surprised to get comments like the one I received after publishing my *"Lead Like a PIRATE* Five Commitments Challenge"*:

Nili—Your enthusiasm inspires us all to try new things and push ourselves a little further than we are comfortable. I feel so lucky to work with you every day. Keep it up, girl! No fear—the time is now!

Split Up the Lead Up

If you are sharing ideas that are perceived as outside of the box or even crazy, you probably feel isolated at times. But if just one other teacher in your school believes in your "crazy idea" as strongly as you do, suddenly it feels easier to share. Do not waste another second. Go find that person. Send them a text or tweet or direct message—now!

Summary

Every personal journey is accompanied by growing pains. They are unavoidable and 100 percent worth it. The growth you experience will put you in a better place. When you decide to put yourself out there and take the leadership plunge, you have to be willing to open the door into unfamiliar territory, but you do not have to go it alone. The next time you find yourself considering a leap of faith, trust the disrupters. They are the visionary voices who will tirelessly support you.

Leadership Treasure Hunt
(Find This)

Find areas of need in your building. Is there a need for enthusiasm? Positivity? Joy? Whatever it is, look for what is missing, feel it, and figure out what it is that is calling your name. It might also be calling the names of others.

Navigating the Seas
(Think about This)

When is the last time you did something despite your fear? When is the last time you didn't do something because of your fear?

Charting the Course
(Take Action)

Think about the situations above, analyze them, and ask yourself what it is about those times that made you either do something or not. Commit to an action that is unlike you, that you would never have considered before becoming a PIRATE. Your stomach might turn, and you might need the support of your PIRATE friends, but it will certainly be worth the ride.

Share your thoughts and ideas!
#LeadLAP

INCITING
CHANGE THROUGH
CONVERSATIONS

Changing culture requires changing the conversations.

—Shelley Burgess and Beth Houf, *Lead Like a PIRATE*

The conversation is the relationship. If the conversation stops, all of the possibilities for the relationship become smaller, and all of the possibilities for the individuals in the relationship become smaller, until one day we over-hear ourselves in midsentence, making ourselves smaller in every encounter, behaving as if we are just the space around our shoes, engaged in yet another three-minute conversation so empty of meaning it crackles.

—Susan Scott, *Fierce Conversations*

It was the second-to-last day of school, and it was pouring outside.
It was a busy day, and perhaps not the best day to ask the school principal for a favor. But Chris Basile, who is one of the second- and third-grade wellness teachers, and I had been discussing *Lead Like a PIRATE* for weeks, and we were excited about the implications of implementing its principles in our school. We had secured personalized, signed copies to give to each of our administrators with the hope of showing our commitment to and belief in our leaders. We wanted them to know that we were there to support them and that we were on the same team. But we wanted to do more than just hand them a copy and say, "Here, from us to you, check out this book!"

That is where the favor came in. We wanted to schedule a formal meeting with our principal. Even though our principal was finishing up bus duty, and it was the worst time possible to meet with her, we reminded ourselves of a favorite quote from Dr. Martin Luther King, Jr.: "The time is always right to do what is right." Chris led the way. People like me bring passion, but we can also be loud (and even repetitive) with our enthusiasm. Sometimes the best decision is to let someone equally passionate initiate the conversation. The beauty in this concept is that, ultimately, it shows whomever it is you are trying to inspire that you are not alone in your thinking or belief.

Fortunately, she was on board with the idea. I am sure she approved, at least in part, because we made such a passionate plea while we all stood in the rain. She also heard our belief and desire: We wanted to empower her to include us in her vision and allow us to join her team. We brought to the table something that was worth fighting for. We joined our principal's team, but just as importantly, she joined ours.

With the meeting scheduling secured, Chris and I had a long conversation the next day about who would say what and why during the meeting. With the plan we had created, we provided for our principal an overview of the book and discussed things such as ideas for building excitement and engagement and for revolutionizing staff meetings. We also listened to her ideas and goals. The energy, humor, and relatability were like nothing I had ever experienced in a meeting before. It turns out our passion and vision were very much in alignment, and for an hour and a half, we talked about the incredible potential that lay ahead. The meeting with our principal kicked off summer break in a powerful way—and she loved the book!

Initiating a conversation about something that mattered to our principal made it easy for her to say yes to our request. If you have an idea or plan, start talking! Invite others to join the conversation and listen to what they have to say. Here are a few more ideas for sparking meaningful conversations:

Grab Attention in Imperfect Situations

If we do not grab our administrators' or colleagues' attention in hallways, the rain, or even the bathroom, we may never do it! It takes courage to walk up to your boss, hand her a leadership book, and say, "Will you meet with me about some ideas for implementing positive change?" You can bet that I was worried that she might feel insulted. But the bigger and better question I had to ask was, *what if she is excited about the idea too?*

If approaching your administrator with requests or ideas seems scary or you worry that your idea may be dismissed because you are the "crazy passionate teacher" who is always pushing ideas, have a colleague join you and let them do the talking. It is hard to ignore two enthusiastic educators who are willing to stand in the rain to talk about the road ahead.

Stay on Target

You owe it to the others in the conversation, and you owe it to your mission to keep the conversation on topic, particularly in a meeting. Keep your goal in front of you right on the table as a constant reminder to stick to your intention, why you are there, and what you can offer. When we get distracted by random thoughts and rabbit trails, it can appear that we lack investment. The more focused your passion, the more that people will believe you can actually do something with it.

Pass the Mic Around

When pitching an idea to positively impact the culture of your building, it is incredibly important that you do not say it all. One person with a crazy idea does not even come close to the power of two people with crazy ideas. But that is not enough. You must make sure the other person does an equal amount of talking if not more. Even when you feel strongly about your ideas, leave space in the conversation for others to talk—and make sure you listen to them.

Summary

Regardless of what people might perceive, and regardless of how things were done before, culture is dramatically better when we are all on the same team. Be intentional about initiating conversations that spark new ideas and empower people to share their thoughts on how to improve your school. No matter your role, it is up to you to make conversations happen.

Leadership Treasure Hunt
(Find This)

Look for opportunities where you can spark
change with a conversation. Find at least one
person to join you in your mission.

 ## Navigating the Seas
(Think about This)

What is the culture of your school right now? What can you
do to contribute to a thriving culture regardless of your title? If
you are already an active contributor, how can you inspire your
colleagues, administrators, and students to do more?

 ## Charting the Course
(Take Action)

Think about the last conversation you had at school that mattered to you and that sparked impact. Whether you initiate a
conversation with your students, colleagues, or administrators,
make sure it is longer than three minutes and full of meaning.

Also make sure that every participant walks away with an
action to take and a commitment to meet again. My principal
was dedicated to reading the book, and Chris and I were dedicated to bringing our passion to our whole school. I have no
doubt that on opening day the following year, Chris and I were
given time to lead our staff because we had all walked away
from our first meeting with a challenge and lived up to it.

Share your thoughts and ideas!
#LeadLAP

The Journey of a PIRATE Educator Who Knows the Power of Communication

Chris Basile, wellness teacher, Elmwood School in Hopkinton, Massachusetts; 2017 MAHPERD Elementary PE Teacher of the Year

When I first started teaching, I believed an effective teacher needed to have passion, a strong belief system, and a trusted support group. I worked on creating all of those things. Now after more than forty years as a teacher, I need to add the fourth cornerstone for effective teaching: communication.

The funny thing is how communication manifests in 2018—compared to say, 1977. The computers, Chromebooks, cell phones, iPads, and touch screens that are commonplace in public school classrooms today were non-existent when I started teaching. In those days, we had blackboards, purple printed mimeo sheets, and film strips projected on a retractable screen, if we were lucky.

I have invested a lot of time improving my content knowledge and teaching skills through the years, but nothing prepared me for the impact technology would make on education during the twenty-first century. The bottom line is, I know my content, but technology humbles me. It makes me nervous sometimes to think about how little I know about the technology that surrounds me. This is why I have added *communication* as a cornerstone to excellent teaching.

The world continues to change, and I know I must develop new skills and resources to remain an effective teacher. To do that, I have worked to understand the role of technology in the lives of my students and to use that technology to connect with my students. I have opened my world and my classroom by using social media to improve my teaching and my connections with my students, my students' teachers, my students' parents, and other educators as well. Communication is fundamental to that connection.

I have learned in the past year how social media can positively impact my teaching. I have experienced firsthand how Twitter, webinars, YouTube, and other forms of social media can prevent teacher burnout by sharing ideas, adding a new twist, encouraging innovation, supporting continued growth, and offering new challenges and solutions. Social media can be used to celebrate, inform, and promote our profession. That is quite a shift in thinking for me because I used to think that social media was used mostly for self-promotion.

I have learned from Nili Bartley about how teachers were using technology to make connections with students, pursue their passions, keep students engaged in class, and create a PLN. The more I have learned and used technology myself to connect with my own amazing PLN, the more I am inspired by the creativity and generosity of teachers around the world. Innovation is a team sport. Communicating and collaborating teachers and students has changed the way I learn—and the way I teach.

USING EMPATHY TO ELEVATE CONVERSATIONS

Think of your company as a beach ball. Picture the beach ball as having a red stripe, a green stripe, a yellow stripe, and a blue stripe. Let's imagine that you are the president of the company. That is you standing on the blue stripe. The blue stripe is where you live, every day, day after day. If someone asks you what color your company is, you look down around your feet and say, "My company is blue."

–Susan Scott, *Fierce Conversations*

I am not a CEO. I do not even hold an administrative title. But I can identify with the "The Beach Ball Effect" as described in the quote above from Susan Scott's book. We all see the stripe we are standing on. That was particularly true for me when I started in my role as technology integration coordinator. The school was composed of a multitude of colors of stripes, but everything I saw was colored by my role. I had not abandoned empathy. I simply thought my initiatives were so important that they seemed more important than the other stripes.

My principal at the second- and third-grade building, on the other hand, does her best to navigate all of the colors. Case in point: School *felt* different when we returned after the summer break. I believe that is largely due to the impact of *Lead Like a PIRATE*. Morning faculty meetings opened each day with teachers sharing something new and exciting. Our principal led the way by asking others to share the amazing things they were doing with students and each other. She often asked questions with genuine curiosity. Everyone was excited to participate. For any staff meeting happening anywhere in the world, those moments are hard to beat.

In our staff meetings and in one-on-one conversations with her, I saw her initiate ideas, push for progress, and empower others to lead. She worked at seeing the whole picture—the whole beach ball. After pleading with her to have a guest speaker come to our school for what I envisioned as an hour of pure empowerment and happiness, her response demonstrated patience and a long-range vision. She explained that as a teacher, she would have jumped at the chance to have the speaker come in, but as a principal, she had more angles to consider. Her answer was not a no; it was a thoughtful pause to consider the needs of everyone in the school.

I want to see past my stripe, and I think I am getting better at it. Empathy is essential because it allows us to continue and deepen conversations. Listening, pausing, and looking at all the angles are just a few skills I have learned from this principal and other PIRATE leaders. Here are a few more ideas to help you elevate conversations and make a greater impact.

See Past Your Stripe

This is so difficult, and sometimes it actually takes being blinded by your own stripe for a while to learn the hard way! Particularly when you are pushing for change, being aware of the needs beyond your own area is so completely worth it. When you go into a conversation with colleagues, administrators, students, and parents, always make sure you are looking for the other stripes. If you are not sure where the people in front of you tend to live, make it a point to find out.

Get to Know the Other Colors

Do not just acknowledge that other colors exist on the beach ball. Get to know them and the people in your building who tend to live in each.

Here is an example: You are at a school event and see happy students getting a drink from the water fountain. You smile as you see the students laughing and talking.

Then you look at your administrator, who is watching the same scene with a look of concern. What she saw first was the puddle of water on the floor. Her concern was about students slipping. Often our leaders live on a stripe where safety is a major focus. Being aware of and willing to address others' concerns, like safety, is important when we bring ideas to them. As awesome and unconventional as our ideas might be, there are many angles we must consider.

Summary

The reality in which we live is not the only one. The more we recognize where others stand, the better leaders we become. It is challenging to get our message across when we do not show an open mind to those in front of us. Beyond anything else, it hurts relationships. At ASCD Empower18, I had the honor of hearing Manny Scott, an original Freedom Writer, author of *How to R.E.A.C.H. Kids Today*, speak about the importance of understanding who we are before we can even attempt to understand the lives of others. It is critical for positive change, and we can all do it with some effort.

Leadership Treasure Hunt
(Find This)

Look for conversations where teachers, administrators, and yes, even our students are clearly living on different beach-ball stripes. Pay attention to the conversations that have the biggest impact and those that have the least.

Navigating the Seas
(Think about This)

Living on your own beach-ball stripe, how often do you think about where others you work with live and what their work life must be like? How often do you consider the daily things they must think about and the goals they strive to reach? If you do not know those things, ask!

Charting the Course
(Take Action)

The next time you meet with your administrators, colleagues, students, or parents, start by looking them in the eyes and asking them how they are. It is simple, but too often ignored, when we are constantly under a time constraint that demands us to get right to the point. Make sure to have an open mind and heart, even when you dare to lead from the front.

Share your thoughts and ideas!
#LeadLAP

STANDING FIRM
IN YOUR BELIEFS

Learning about what we don't understand helps
us reduce anxiety, as does having colleagues
and partners with whom we can work through
challenges and celebrate success.

–Shelley Burgess and Beth Houf, *Lead Like a PIRATE*

My name is Tenacity Tiger. My superpower
is perseverance. When I persevere, I
empower others to never give up.

–Maura (aka, Tenacity Tiger)

The SuperPIRATES of Crew 202 and I believed that we could be whoever we chose to be. To that end, we chose superhero names and referred to ourselves and one another by those names. It was a simple act that meant something important to all of us.

Every time we called out a student by his or her superhero name and every time students wrote their names on their papers, those words reminded us all of the traits we claimed. "Tenacity Tiger," for example, was fiercely determined. I chose the name "Lioness PIRATE" and declared I would use my wish superpower of courage to encourage others around me to take risks. When others in the school questioned our use of the super-charged names or hinted that we lived in a pretend world, our determination to live like PIRATES only got stronger—and our results only got better. We believed in ourselves and in one another.

My WHY is empowering others. That is what I was doing with my students as a teacher, and it is what I wanted to do with the educators I served as a technology integration coordinator. But honestly, sometimes creating empowerment opportunities within the walls of one's own building can be tricky, and getting everyone on board can be challenging, especially when change is required.

When I defined my role, I was suddenly no longer locked in the technology lab. That was great for me, but more than one teacher mentioned right before the new school year started, "I really wish you were in the computer lab so we could still come down once a week for technology. Any chance that will happen again? At least then I had a set time."

I could have backed down from my vision of empowering teachers to integrate technology into their classroom—rather than relegating technology to the computer lab. But I did not, and as a result, those same teachers are now rocking their students' worlds with lessons that use technology in incredibly meaningful ways. I did not let myself down and, in turn, did not let them down because I chose to defend my role. The first time I heard that question, I replied, almost without having to think about it, "It is not about signing up for me to bring technology class to your room. It is about *you* bringing purposeful technology into your classroom to elevate the impact of your lessons. My mission is to help get you there, and I will."

I am the one who created the change in the way I worked to fulfill my WHY, and I knew that if I could sell teachers on WHY by standing firm in my beliefs, then they would give me a chance to show them HOW. So that is what I did.

Whatever your WHY is and whatever the changes are that need to happen to make your vision a reality, you can count on getting some pushback. Here are a few ideas to help you defend your decisions and stand firm in your beliefs:

Stay Strong No Matter What

Under no circumstances (as long as everything you are doing is legal and appropriate) should you back down! Your WHY can stand up to questioning; it is too strong not to. From trying unconventional approaches in the classroom to shaking things up with teachers, I could have easily given in to make others happy or less concerned. Years ago, I put service learning on hold until after state testing because I did not want to upset my colleagues. I soon realized that was a big mistake **because the most important people I was serving, my students, missed out.**

Provide Evidence of Current Practices

Tell them your decision was based on best practices. It was clear to me that our lab was rather outdated and not conducive to twenty-first-century learning, but not everyone knew that. My job, then, was to educate people about best practices and my reasoning for the change. When someone questions your methods, help them understand by providing education and evidence to support your decisions. The more people know, the less they assume. That is good for you because unfortunately, when change comes zooming in, most people fear it and assume the worst until they understand it.

Determine the Origin of Doubt

Ask your colleagues and even your students why they are worried or dislike the change they are faced with. Seeking to understand their fears can open the doors to better relationships. I learned, for example, that one particular colleague was not "there" yet with technology, but she wanted to be. To her, that "tech time" in the lab helped her become familiar with digital tools and increased her confidence in using them. This was so important for me to know! I was able to model lessons in her classroom and meet with her one-on-one to discuss blending lessons and units with a focus on using just two to three tools. Over time, she mastered the tools and felt like a rock star!

Summary

When I defined my role based on my WHY, my passion and belief in what I was doing became even stronger. It became easier then to stand up for my decisions. My dedication and belief helped people trust me more. We can use our roles to impact the culture of a school, but for the greatest impact, we must share how our role will positively affect the roles of others. We must connect to them, show belief in them, and follow through whole heartedly with our mission.

Leadership Treasure Hunt
(Find This)

When change takes place, we know people will talk. Do not wait for them to come to you. Go out there and immerse yourself in conversations so you can dispel doubts before they spread.

Navigating the Seas
(Think about This)

When is the last time you defended something while talking to your colleagues, administrators, or even yourself? Why did you defend it, and what was the outcome?

Charting the Course
(Take Action)

The next time someone questions something you are doing or about to try, defend it with your WHY. Share the positive impact you believe is about to transpire because of your new course of action. Sell your belief.

Share your thoughts and ideas!
#LeadLAP

PUTTING YOUR WORDS INTO ACTION

Hope alone doesn't create change. Action does.

—Shelley Burgess and Beth Houf, *Lead Like a PIRATE*

I smile to everyone to make sure everyone is motivated.

—Kylie

I am making sure that I matter in 2016 by not forgetting my superpower–being bold. I've been taking a lot of risks and am not afraid to stand up for myself anymore!

—Angie

I used my superpower when a kid at my camp was bullying someone, and I stood up to the bully, and he stopped.

—Kyle

I noticed that since I identified my superpower, I felt a change in everything! I have been more positive and a lot more happy with who I am.

—Libby

When I was a freshman athlete at Boston University some twenty years ago, the coaches awed me. (And a few struck me with fear!) Chris Basile was the women's basketball coach and someone I deeply admired. Although we spoke only a handful of times at BU, she made a statement that stuck with me throughout college and rang again in my mind at the beginning of the 2017–2018 school year: "The time is now." Chris is the teacher who had been beside me that rainy day at the end of the previous school year. She returned to teaching after her college coaching career, and I believe it is PIRATE fate that brought us together.

The time was upon us. Our principal had been so impressed by what she heard from us during our meeting that she agreed to give us fifteen minutes to share our passion and vision during the first PD day before school started that fall. I knew we had to include "the time is now" in our presentation. It was important to Chris to share the value of staying in the moment as this is what the best athletes do. We both wanted to share the value of bringing passion to school *now* for ourselves, for each other, and for our students. We took a risk and shared our stories (much of it unscripted, which made it even better!).

As we played the "Top Three" activity from *Lead Like a PIRATE*, I looked around the room. I realized our colleagues were truly engaged in the moment. Choosing three favorite movies and identifying a common theme was a lot more challenging for them than we had anticipated. It occurred to us that our colleagues had probably not been asked to get in touch with what they care deeply about in the school setting. That was about to change.

In those moments, we all experienced the feeling of being a team. From the PE teacher to technology and classroom teachers to guidance counselors and administrators, it did not matter what our titles were; we were all just human beings thinking about who we are and what we live for. I knew then that the biggest change was not going to be the shift from the lab to the classroom. It would be my level of investment. I knew that if I was really going to empower my colleagues and help each of them unleash their own passion and purpose, I would have to be all in with *my* passion and purpose. My actions had to back up my words, every day.

In the following day's PD session, I took it one step further. It was important that my colleagues saw that what Chris and I had brought to them the previous day was not just talk. Through my movie choices and transparency at school, I had demonstrated my passion for helping people understand what they could do or be. I decided to take the demonstration a step further when I was given fifteen minutes to introduce my new role. Rather than focus on schedules and outlines, I talked about my mindset. Colleen Worrell taught me her 5Cs of a tech integration coach: coteacher, collaborator, consultant, colleague, and coach. I've adopted those 5Cs and added two more: connector and catalyst. For this session, the word catalyst seemed like the perfect focus for explaining my redefined role. I told the teachers and administrators that day that I was committed to sparking change and launching a year of teacher leadership. As I shared my goals for my role as a technology integration specialist, I focused on the word *catalyst*. I explained that I wanted to be a catalyst every single day. I promised to work relentlessly to spark change and even get out of the way of their passionate work that would continue to brew without me.

What happened next was planned yet unanticipated at the same time. A second-grade teacher in the group talked about a simple tech tip I had shared with her the year before when she had come to me looking for new ways to reach her students. She needed something motivational and engaging that would involve an audience, ideally families. Seesaw was the first tool that came to my mind. Less than a year later, this amazing colleague had become a Seesaw Ambassador. I was thrilled when she asked our principal for permission to lead an interactive PD session for staff all about how to use Seesaw. By sharing about her own teacher-leader experience at the meeting that day—and acknowledging my role as a catalyst for her—she offered evidence to our colleagues that I would support *them* in their efforts to change, grow, and lead.

Here are a few ideas that will help you put your words into action:

Launch the Year in Front of Staff

It does not matter if you get ten minutes or two. Being face to face makes an impact, and if you can get a colleague to share something revolutionary with you (like passion in school!), it will be ten times more powerful. Preparing for your face-to-face time is a precious piece of the puzzle so go at it hard-core. I chose to create Google Slides exploding with quotes and images from *Empower* by A.J. Juliani and John Spencer. I challenged teachers to consider the ladder of compliance, engagement, and empowerment and asked them which rung they would rather be on. Giving them something they could hold onto like "The 7 Cs" was invaluable, and everyone digested it at the exact same moment.

Jump on Opportunities for Colleagues to Fight for You

If a colleague is able to exemplify how your role contributed to change, jump on that opportunity like there's no tomorrow! When I found out my Seesaw Ambassador was getting an hour in front of staff, I asked her if it would be okay to create a quick introduction at the beginning. I also asked her to be the one to ask our principal, who had already approved her presentation. This was not because I was afraid my principal would say no if I was the one who asked. It was because if a teacher asks an administrator to allow for her colleague to take up some of her time, that shows *a lot* about how much she respects that particular colleague and his or her role. For an administrator to see this come to life, well, that is everything.

Sell It by Doing

We cannot assume that teachers catch every email, tip, inspirational post, picture, and quote we send. When someone *does* ask for more information or for you to explain what you're doing and why, jump at the chance to share! When you do, you can be sure that teachers will talk with others about what they're learning from you. As teachers signed up for me to come into their class or to meet with them one on one, change began to happen and spread. The first couple of months alone drove more purposeful technology in classrooms than the previous two years combined.

Summary

Showing up with your actions (not just your words) inspires and encourages others. Actions give your statements the power to build the kind of trust that transforms learning for students, staff, and administrators. Show up at every PLC. Share ideas. Listen to uncover the needs of your colleagues.

As I thought about ways to put my words in to action, I changed what had started the year before as "Delicious Demos" (a time for me to talk about apps and devices in the classroom) to "Coffee and Conversation" to let my colleagues know that I valued their voices too. I switched up the topics based on others' interests. I have gotten to know colleagues on a personal level inside and outside of school by allowing them time to share. We feel more like a crew, now, and *that's* a game changer for PIRATEs.

Leadership Treasure Hunt
(Find This)

Find opportunities to share who you are and what you have to offer. Just make sure to back up what you are preaching with action.

Navigating the Seas
(Think about This)

If you asked your students and/or staff to explain how you define your role, what do you think they would say? If you asked your students and/or staff to explain what you do that makes them believe in you, what do you think they would they say?

Charting the Course
(Take Action)

It is important to define your role, but asking students and staff to define it is just as important. Go out there and ask them! If you are a bit hesitant, you might be questioning whether you have been backing your words up with action. Recognizing room for improvement is a good thing and getting input from those you serve may well lead to necessary transformation. You have got this!

Share your thoughts and ideas!
#LeadLAP

BUILDING YOUR CREW OF COLLEAGUES

Your crew is essential to the survival of your building
and the success of your students.

—Shelley Burgess and Beth Houf, *Lead Like a PIRATE*

All pirates travel with a crew; you can't sail, navigate,
and fight battles all on your own.

—Dave Burgess

Being part of a crew this year makes me feel like I'm a part
of something. Being a "specialist" can get lonely, and it is
easy to feel stagnant. Being in a crew gave me a sense of
community, which made me more excited about my work
and gave me the courage to take more risks (for example,
with technology) and to share what I'm doing.

—Bonnie Gaus, colleague

The SuperPIRATES of Crew 202 taught me that with enough passion and enthusiasm, building a crew of students who are willing to join new adventures with you is not only doable, but a lot of fun. I felt the same way (and always will) about my far away crew—my PLN. Thanks to social media, Google Hangouts, and the good fortune of meeting many in person, I have bonded with educators all over the country who I know would have my back. I would tweet the risks I was trying, the experiences that I could not believe were unfolding right in front of my eyes, and invariably, someone would respond with encouragement or advice.

Today, whether it is #TLAP, #LeadLAP, #LeadLAPmass, or any of the other hashtags I follow, it is still the human beings behind these hashtags who provide camaraderie. They give me something to believe in that is bigger than myself. When I discovered Twitter chats, I found a sporting event for my brain *and* a way to make new friends. The online PLN I connected with offered immediate support when I launched my personal PIRATE journey as an educator. That support has only grown through the years. We all need that connection and support as unconventional educators.

When I left the classroom, I needed to build a new crew for daily, in-person connection. It did not happen overnight. At times I depended so much on my far away crew that I forgot to tap into the power of a crew within the walls of the buildings I worked in each day. That changed when I started to collaborate with the teachers and administrators around me. Now I feel as if I have finally found a misfit crew of colleagues I am convinced will never jump ship—regardless of how unconventional I might seem to others. My crewmates do not share every single one of my passions, but they share the desire to be passionate in their work.

One of the things that strengthened our bond was attending a conference together. For us, it was MassCUE. Prior to the conference,

> My crewmates do not share every single one of my passions, but they share the desire to be passionate in their work.

I went around the school convincing my crewmates that they "had" to go. I already knew they would be excited about the opportunity for new learning. We dubbed ourselves MassCUE Crew. The conference sessions focused on empathy, empowerment, growth mindset, and global change, and we soaked up every word. We came back inspired to share the themes and what we had learned from the sessions that embraced them. We bonded over ideas we could not wait to implement. I felt such a deep appreciation for my crew because, for the first time ever, teachers from my school had seen me leading a session on my PIRATE journey. This meant everything.

We solidified the purpose of our crew by making sure everyone around us knew that we were a united team ready to accept new players any time. Had we isolated ourselves, we may have created resentment and would have failed in our mission to empower others to pursue their passions as educators. So we made it a point to say, "We are here. Come join us!" Doing so eliminated chances of isolation and increased the opportunity for camaraderie district wide.

Here are a few simple ideas to build your crew of colleagues and make it strong:

Trust Your Gut

If your instinct tells you that you could make an even stronger impact by connecting with certain people, do it! If you know people who are craving new learning and would do anything to make the time for it (yes, even if that means writing sub notes for two whole days), go after them, and convince them that you have a way for them to satisfy their craving. Spend as much time as possible bonding with each of them. You will not regret it. There is absolutely nothing in the world like having people who have your back.

Share Yourselves as an Open Roster

Whether it is a conference or conversation, whatever takes place that sparks your crew, make a commitment to be open about who you are and share with your colleagues what bonds you. During our staff meeting "share," we decided to each bring a part of our MassCUE experience back to our colleagues. Whether it was new video creation apps, coding tools, twenty-first-century spaces, or one hot book study on Twitter for Massachusetts educators called #LeadLAPmass, we made it clear that the excitement we have for increasing student empowerment is more important than the specific tools we used to achieve that goal. Our passion is what brought us together. We knew if we could communicate our enthusiasm, we would connect to the heart and inspire those around us to join our mission.

Show Faith in Those Around You

I began the share by looking my colleagues and administrators in the eyes and expressing how I was so proud to work with individuals whom I can challenge to capitalize on what they're already doing, who will listen to me say, "We need to meet our kids where they are as well as where they are headed." I asked them to accept a shift in mindset because the amount of technology we have access to will never be more important than giving students *real-life* opportunities to use it. I made a point to meet teachers where *they* were and to hook them into considering where their students are, even just at eight and nine years old. Audience, connection, empowerment. This set the tone for the whole presentation as something they could be a part of, and even lead, with us. When you present yourself as a crew, you must convey your purpose and invite others in.

Bring a Question

At the end of the conference, we high-fived, hugged, and shared a deeper belief in our purpose as educators. We came back with a question for our colleagues and administrators: "What can we do?" We said it, displayed it, and asked them to act on it. Just like with our students, we must hook teachers and administrators with empowerment and mean it.

Keep Your Mission Relevant

Unfortunately, too often we hear about something horrible in the news and then head to a staff meeting later that day or the next to discuss what seems like minutia. I was feeling scared and overwhelmingly sad with the ongoing violence in our country, so I chose to lead our crew in the faces of others with transparency, vulnerability, and determination to make a difference. I told them I doubted there was a person in the room who didn't wake up in the morning thinking about the state of our country, that we weren't here to talk about technology from a technology conference but a mindset that would allow us to ask our kids to change the world, or like Colleen Worrell says, "make it suck less." There is nothing that will connect to people in a room more than being real, relevant, and motivational.

Put the Voices of Your Crew in the Spotlight

Even if your crewmates cannot attend an event with you, turn those creative wheels on and make sure their voices are heard. Knowing Chris could not be there for our MassCUE presentation that special morning staff meeting, it was a no-brainer. I would video her and project her magnetism for everyone to see. As she shared her captivating social media journey, her message reached us within seconds.

Becoming a connected educator will not only change our lives but the lives of our students. Check out Chris's amazing video here! (bit.ly/ChrisBasile) Each colleague after Chris, in her own unique way, continued to speak with excitement and humor, yet at the same time conveyed importance and even a sense of urgency. The audience was captivated as each speaker changed, and the brilliance of what transpired was that I never spoke again during our share. I did not have to.

Summary

Building the MassCUE Crew was, without a doubt, the best educational decision I have made in the past three years. For the first time, not only did it hit me that I was not alone, but I knew I would never be alone again. During our share, I actually found myself in unfamiliar territory as, for the first time ever, it was a colleague who passionately discussed sessions that I happened to lead. It was humbling to say the least, but when you build a crew of colleagues who have your back no matter how unconventional you get, who believe in a mission you have created together, and who tirelessly support you, be ready for this to happen to you too.

Leadership Treasure Hunt
(Find This)

Find those people in your building or district you
know would jump on your ship in a heartbeat.
Find something for you to bond over. If not a conference, at least start with a conversation.

 # Navigating the Seas
(Think about This)

If you already have a crew, what bonded you? How do you
continue to energize the glue that holds you together?

 # Charting the Course
(Take Action)

Once you find and build your crew, meet with them often.
Make sure you identify what you stand for, why you are in it
to win it together. Determine the steps you can take so that
you stick together. Your agenda and strategies may change, but
your desire to bring your WHY should always guide your ship.

The Journey of a PIRATE
Teacher Who Found Her Crew

Dena O'Shaughnessy, third-grade teacher,

Hopkinton, Massachusetts

Every day is different, and as I pull into the parking lot of our elementary school each morning in the darkness, hours before the students arrive, I feel a sense of excitement about what the day holds. Crazy as it may sound to some, I look forward to reviewing my lessons, planning and tweaking, reflecting, and differentiating for each third grader in my class, before most of my colleagues arrive.

While I have always loved my job, this sense of anticipation and excitement is new. What has caused this transformation? I have found my "crew." Or maybe I should say we have found each other. Though most have us have worked together for the past ten or so years, we worked in isolation. We were not aware that we shared the same feelings and teaching philosophy.

I have always loved taking professional-development classes, attending seminars, researching, and reading books related to the latest trends in teaching. However, I often felt alone in my enthusiasm to try new things. Then in a casual conversation one day with Nili, I mentioned that I had been reading and researching passion projects and Genius Hour and was considering having my third graders embark on this journey.

Immediately, she broke into a huge smile and told me that she had done it the previous year with her fourth graders, I should absolutely do it, and it would be one of the best things I had ever done with my kiddos. I could not believe it! I was absolutely thrilled! She assured me she would help me, and she followed through on that promise. Nili even invited some of her past students to come in to my classroom, chat with my students, and answer their questions.

The support and encouragement I received from Nili and the other PIRATES around me has helped me understand that taking risks is a good thing, especially if it is in the interest of student learning. I now feel an incredible sense of empowerment. The bit of self-doubt and anxiety that had been dwelling in the back of my brain has gone.

I am so thankful to have found a crew of teachers from different areas of the building who are all excited to collaborate and support one another. Wherever you are, find *your* crew. Their support will have you running into school each day, even if it is in the wee hours of the morning!

From Building
a Crew to
Expanding It

How could you ensure that if your staff didn't have
to be there, the room would still be full?

—Shelley Burgess and Beth Houf, *Lead Like a PIRATE*

If I had asked people what they wanted,
they would have said faster horses.

—Henry Ford

A **"culture of yes" is the ideal that we should all aim to reach together.** What I have found, however, is that sometimes we exist in cultures that are not asking enough questions. Sometimes teachers and administrators honestly do not know what to ask or do not know what is out there that is worth asking for. They have not been exposed to enough revolutionary ideas to become inspired enough to try them. They need a time to talk, learn, ask, and act.

I love listening to IMMOOC episodes with George Couros and Katie Martin, because I have the opportunity to hear powerful (and often entertaining) conversations unfold. By the end of each, I'm always left with the same question: "What can *I* do?" When you are not an administrator, answering this question becomes more challenging but far from impossible. Here are just a couple of lines from one of my favorite IMMOOC interviews with Joe Sanfelippo and Tony Sinanis. It is one I come back to often.

> **Katie Martin:** "If we're really creating meaningful experiences for teachers that shift their thinking, that shift their experiences . . . what are some tangible things that we can take back to our own context?"
>
> **Tony Sinanis:** "I think first and foremost, we need to give teachers time to collaborate."

I learned from the SuperPIRATES of Crew 202 the power in giving kids time to talk about what matters to them. The motivation for learning explodes. I believe this is also true when initiating conversations with our peers. We want to talk about what matters, own our learning, and most certainly bring our experiences right back to our students. I wanted more than anything to bring an unconventional experience to our building. I had shifted the typical staff meeting at the K–1 building with much success. It was time for second- and third-grade staff to have a similar opportunity, only we would go bigger. We would go PIRATE.

At a recent *Lead Like a PIRATE* Edcamp session Colleen and I had decided to lead, a heart-racing, jump-out-of-your-seat conversation had erupted. How often does this happen in our buildings? How often do we make it happen? I was inspired to make it happen in mine. Although it would be mini, modified, and optional, Chris and I put our heads together and were supported to make an Edcamp experience happen.

Motivated by *The Power of Moments* by Chip Heath and Dan Heath (and I had only just begun!), I was determined to look for defining moments that made our #edcampsemass conversation what it was so that I could make memorable moments for my colleagues. I did not have to think too hard. About halfway through our session, Brian McCann, principal of Case High School in Swansea, Massachusetts, said the following: "I'm not asking permission to be awesome, and I'm not apologizing for being passionate."

This statement broke the ice for all of us. The second those words came out of Brian's mouth, I knew I was in the right place at the right time that day, as well as in my career. It gave us a push to unleash who we are, trust each other, and share our thinking. This is what Edcamp is all about. After much reflection, I decided the "moment" I would spark for staff and administrators would be the actual experience.

It was important to hype up a couple of things before the big day: PIRATE and the power of conversation. I met with my colleagues who committed to leading or exploring a topic and made sure they felt prepared to be unprepared. I encouraged them to honor the

I was simply providing the fuel and letting them drive. And they most certainly did.

discussions that would unfold. I was simply providing the fuel and letting them drive. And they most certainly did.

Teachers, as well as my principal, dove into meaningful conversations around social emotional learning strategies, Breakout EDU, video creation apps, Seesaw, the PIRATE revolution, and Genius Hour, which included Thrively and Ignite Your S.H.I.N.E.®. Although it was mini, modified, and optional, on December 18th from 3:30 to 5:00, Chris and I created an Edcamp experience. Because it was high on their priority list, teachers took with them something they could try with their students the very next day. Most had walked in with only an idea of what to expect and went home that afternoon craving more.

Here are a few simple ideas that will make your Edcamp Style PD amazing!

Sell it Early, Often, and Unconventionally!

Chris and I came up with a catchy slogan to help us sell "Elmwood Edcamp": "Remember December!" We created video advertisements and purposefully only did raw takes. We knew that if we were bringing something unconventional, we needed to sell it unconventionally, and it worked. Full of mistakes, our videos carried this message: On December 18th, at our teacher choice staff meeting, teachers would be given a voice—the whole time. Check our original unconventional advertisement video here! (bit.ly/edcampad1)

Push for Passion Pep Talks

There is nothing like letting teachers know they have immediate support from exceptional educators who not only bring their passion to work daily but have certainly found their purpose. I reached out to a few of my PIRATE friends, and "Passion Pep Talks" were born. Not only were they a big hit, but bringing far away crewmates into my building virtually connected all of us together in a way I had not experienced. It also provided evidence that this whole PIRATE thing is the real deal and allowed for teachers to add their own! This is still a work in progress, but we must never ever give up. Check out amazing Passion Pep talks right here and feel free to add your own! (flipgrid.com/738ee7 Password—Passion1)

Decorate the Heck out of Your Space

It is important that teachers (and administrators!) are lured into using all five senses when providing them with professional development. If we really want our colleagues to grow with each other, they must see, taste, smell, touch, and hear the theme so they are not only energized but have absolutely no doubt in their mind the WHY behind the experience about to unfold. We had PIRATE-themed decorations, snacks, and a lot of coffee; twenty colleagues showed up to the library ready to learn.

Let the Words of Others Do Most of the Talking

We fail miserably when we deliver the message of promoting teacher voice and talk the majority of the time. I will never forget our first staff day a few years ago. Well intentioned, our leadership team began with a famous quote that we all know from Angela Maiers: "You matter." I was pumped and then immediately deflated as for the next three hours, we did nothing but our best to listen and watch PowerPoints. Needless to say, at our Edcamp, I chose to speak very little. I shared Tony Sinanis's thoughts about collaborating, replayed the end of one of the most exciting Patriots games ever (ironic that the Patriots make it in again!), and thanks to *The Power of Moments*, left teachers hungry to discuss this question: "What is the game for students?"

Have the Time of Your Life

In *Lead with Culture*, Jay Billy writes about his school and, how "All staff feel empowered to make joyful moments and share the fun with others." Imagine if this were a goal in every building. Honestly, if you don't have fun, what is the point? It hit me during our Edcamp experience: the value in bonding over laughs, particularly when administrators are in the room. It is good for the soul, and it is good for relationships. I have learned it is also incredible for productivity. Yet the bottom line that we must pay attention to is that an experience like this does not happen without people willing to lead and have fun right along with you and, in this case, lead more.

No One Leaves Without Feedback!

Whether it is through a survey, video interviews, whatever it takes, feedback is a must! It is essential that you document how people felt about the experience. Do not just get the feedback. Immediately take it to your administrators and share it. Dare to ask the most important question one could possibly ask after an incredible experience. When can we do this again? If you do not take that chance and if you do not push for more teacher-led opportunities, you end up isolating an hour-and-a-half event that slides into the trap of being forgotten.

Check out some feedback below.

There is no better way to learn than from your colleagues! Thank you to everyone who shared—it was a great experience, and I learned a lot!

I loved learning more about such exciting opportunities. It was so great to talk to my colleagues and to share their excitement—and my own!

I loved the enthusiasm brought today. Such a great change of pace, and it was engaging. I would love to be able to do something like this again!

Summary

Authentic conversations matter, and we must spark them as often as possible. I will indeed "Remember December" because my crew expanded. The four colleagues who took a risk to lead our staff through an hour of unconventional PD that they had little experience with put their trust in me and vice versa. They knocked it out of the park, showing their colleagues and administrators that it was possible to sail beyond their titles and lead beyond the classroom. That special day sparked a culture of teachers sharing in new ways. Whether through face-to-face discussions, pineapple charts, Twitter, our one-word challenge, and more, it happened, and it is still happening. It even encouraged me to try a similar experience in the other building, and I am thrilled to say the same contagious energy was ignited. In fact, it is after this experience when I received from a kindergarten teacher what I believe to be the best PD compliment ever: "Great ideas! Cannot wait to use them in my classroom! I would buy a ticket to this PD!"

Leadership Treasure Hunt
(Find This)

Become an authentic conversation detective before, during, and after school. Celebrate each time you witness colleagues sharing what matters to them and work relentlessly to keep this culture going!

Navigating the Seas
(Think about This)

Have you ever attended Edcamp? Have you ever brought it to your staff? How could you make it happen?

Charting the Course
(Take Action)

Intentionally carve out time to meet with at least one colleague to spark a conversation around what matters to them and what matters to you. Come up with ideas that honor your passions and take a risk by putting even one idea into action. The results may shock you.

Pushing for Professional Growth

If we are truly serious about creating the culture of getting our students and staff running in rather than out, we have to be willing to transform our daily practices.

–Shelley Burgess and Beth Houf, *Lead Like a PIRATE*

Teachers create what they experience.

–Katie Martin, *Learner-Centered Innovation*

I learned from the SuperPIRATES of Crew 202 that, as educators, we cannot "one and done" impactful learning. We must look at what is working well and continue the heck out of it. Our Elmwood Edcamp was so impactful, that to me, it seemed clear that sharing and effective PD needed to play more significant roles in the culture of our building. So, in PIRATE fashion, I arranged a meeting with my principal, showed her the feedback, and asked the following question: How can we keep this excitement for learning going? Instead of just asking, I decided to become part of the answer.

Keeping Katie Martin's quote in mind, I felt that although my administrators listened to me, meeting every so often was not enough. I needed to get more creative, and I knew having a professional development or leadership team could give teachers a voice in how we learn as well as keep the culture of sharing going strong. I had brought it up before, but sometimes you just have to be that squeaky wheel, especially when you know you have something worth fighting for. The last time I was looking to make a change, I typed it all up, the WHY, HOW, and WHAT. So I did the exact same thing.

Goal of Potential PD Team (WHY)

- To discuss revolutionary practices in education and how we can bring them to each other so we can bring them to our students.

Hope (HOW)

- To work with principals once a month to discuss how to bring new learning experiences into PD time.

A PD Team could be used for ... (WHAT)

- Discussing PLC time as a golden opportunity for teacher-driven conversations around data and best practices
- Creating innovative ways to structure PLC staff meetings
- Helping to structure PD days
- Helping to create surveys in order to differentiate learning experiences for teachers
- Exploring getting best use out of Pineapple Chart
- Discussing using Twitter to not only share what is happening in our classrooms but to grow professionally.
- Offering ideas to help structure staff meetings

Examples of PD approaches/practices ...

- **Genius Hour for Teachers**: Certain time carved out every month to research what we are passionate about—could be attached to our professional goal.
- **Edcamp Style PD**: Open up time to have authentic conversations and teach each other in a workshop model.
- **Flipped Meeting**: Have us look at something beforehand and come ready to discuss a video, five minutes of reading, etc.
- **Pecha Kucha**: Have a six-minute ignite session with a chit chat after. This is incredibly impactful.
- **Breakout EDU**: Teachers uncover the content through working together to solve clues—we have kits, and there are teachers who could set one up called Staff Meeting.
- **Tech Apps to Introduce/Reflect on Content:** For example, use Quizlet LIVE—get teachers playing a game in teams to learn the content you wish to deliver. Use PADLET to express knowledge in our preferred learning styles and comment on one another's posts. Launch Google Classroom or Google+

Community to communicate w/teachers. Have them share before, during, and after PD.

- **QR Code Scavenger Hunt:** Have us find/answer questions about the content around the room linked to QR codes.
- **PE Connection**: Do a PE activity in the gym, learning new movement breaks to help students to gain learning readiness skills.
- **Wellness/SEL:** Have us walk in assessing what zone we are in and practice strategies students are learning to be ready for learning (green). Have the afternoon meeting set up like morning meeting to start staff meetings when possible.
- **Student-Led PD:** Invite students to present and coach us with new technology tools.
  - **TONS of quick ideas to structure meetings:** Draw from *Four O'clock Faculty, Lead Like a PIRATE*, and *Learner-Centered Innovation,* from ice breakers to demos to full-length PD time. In fact, this is a great post I just saw from a Twitter chat that the *Four O'Clock Faculty* author led where Massachusetts principals shared their PD ideas:(fouroclockfaculty.com/2018/06/10-pd-ideas).

I gave this to my principals at the very end of the year. It is not perfect. It is not incredibly organized, but it could not wait any longer. Sometimes urgency takes over perfection, and you just need to run with it. I also decided to up my game of sharing with colleagues and get them sharing with each other, and this has made all of the difference.

Here are a few ideas, in addition to going big with the ones above, so that you can make sharing and professional growth a more significant part of your culture.

Focus on What, Not Who

As someone who loves to read and listen to podcasts, I have worked hard over the past year to inspire my colleagues by bringing them revolutionary practices. My most recent attempt at this was an idea inspired by *Four O'Clock Faculty* by Rich Czyz I called "Coffee and Conversation." What I learned was that it does not matter how many show up. What matters is who you have in front of you and what you accomplish together. Aim for one person to join you in going rogue, and you will be amazed at the results.

When the Number is 0, Get Creative

You cannot dwell on zero people showing up to something you are launching or zero people using the pineapple chart as a negative. Sure, the question, "How can you reach teachers?" becomes more challenging to answer, but it is far from impossible. It just means it is time to get more creative, so ask yourself what you can do with the constraints you have, and you might just be shocked.

Here are a few ways I have worked at being creative with reaching teachers.

Create Quick Videos

I knew my colleagues certainly desired to learn and share, but I needed to get more creative. Suddenly one-minute-and-twenty-three-second videos were born. If I could manage to do something quick yet impactful, something that had my voice without me talking (I knew I would talk too much!), and maybe even add a little music, I might get people watching. I knew that if I could make that happen, two things would follow: sparking interest and igniting authentic conversations. The next day began with, "Hey, I saw your video!" It does not necessarily matter when the conversations happen. Just get them going! Here are a couple of videos I recently put together with QuickTime and iMovie (two oldies but goodies).

- Coffee and Conversation: Why Join the
  Educational Revolution of PIRATE books and
  Podcasts? (bit.ly/PIRATErev)
- Coffee and Conversation: Why
  Passion? (bit.ly/WHYPassion)

Tip: When you go for creating videos, be yourself, be sure to add humor, and keep in mind that it is not just students who like to catch mistakes. Adults love it too, so do not correct all of them. It keeps you human, and it gets them smiling.

Plaster Pineapple Pics

If you have a pineapple chart, celebrate it, launch its debut, and invite principals to model first. I even encourage eating a pineapple or drinking pineapple juice and playing some Hawaiian music. Put it in a space where *everyone* can see. Unfortunately, the grand debut kickoff never quite happened for us, and folks were reluctant to use it. So instead of focusing on only getting teachers into one another's classrooms, I decided to take a step back and focus first on promoting the risk of putting our names up there. That is what my colleagues needed. Not only did I frequently say, "Whoa, you're going to pineapple that, right?" (Yes, we used it as a verb.) I also made sure to take pictures of any "pineappled" lessons or events and plaster them all over the wall right next to the pineapple chart, titled, "In case you missed it." Even when something is created with a specific purpose, we must step back and nurture the process. I have no doubt teachers will be rocking the pineapple chart next year, and you can too!

Push into What Already Exists

When you are trying to go rogue and especially when you are struggling for time, push your idea into something that already exists. When I heard about book tastings from Rich Czyz, I immediately reached out to our committee that runs staff breakfasts once a month and asked if I could use a few tables for a PIRATE book tasting. I had a big visible sign-out chart, so everyone could see what everyone else was signing out in hopes that my colleagues would take notice of what others were interested in. I also hoped it would spark conversation. It did!

Create a PD Library

From the book tasting came a small but powerful PD library, and I highly suggest creating one and putting it, like the pineapple chart, in a place where teachers walk by every single day. Do not stop there. Push yourself to get to know your colleagues so well that you can recommend the perfect book for them! Also, by the library, hang quotes about professional development, links to podcasts, and more! Anything to grab attention! Bathrooms and refrigerators are also great locations for anything you would like teachers to see!

Tap into the Power of Paras

The paraprofessionals I have had the honor of working with are honestly gold for our buildings. I had the pleasure of leading a Google PD for them with a brilliant colleague. We decided together that relevancy would come first, that we would make it worthwhile, and it was a great success. In fact, they had never been so excited about a half day in their educational lives and could not stop thanking us. Many went home to continue using Google Drawings, Calendar, Drive, and more. Why don't we tap into the power of paraprofessionals as often as possible? They can teach the teachers they work with, who often have overflowing plates! Why not? Be the one in your building to make this happen!

Go Big with Book Studies

I met with a colleague recently and asked what she thought about launching a book study on *Learner-Centered Innovation*. I was thinking just teachers in my building, and she said, "Nili, think bigger." So I met with our superintendent, and she not only gave me her undivided attention but also gave her endorsement whole-heartedly. We were eighteen strong in a district-wide summer book study (advertised through video, of course: bit.ly/bookstudyad) using Google Classroom. I had hoped the book study would be hopping with excitement, which would lead to a Twitter chat and a face-to-face meet-up at the end. We didn't get quite that far, but the study lit a spark and led to great conversations, and that meant everything. All because I listened to a colleague, who happens to have amazing ideas, and took her advice. I encourage you to initiate a book study for your school or district. Go big!

Summary

As Jimmy Casas discusses in *Culturize*, behavior defines our ability to lead, not our titles. We can all do it, and when we experience something powerful in education, we must look at it as our responsibility to keep it going. "One and done" is not enough. It may take putting it all out there on paper, taking risks with leading colleagues and administrators in unconventional ways, and pushing ourselves to get more creative than we thought possible—especially when the odds are against us! Come back to how you define yourself. For me, it was those 7 Cs, and I focused mostly on *catalyst*. I could not let my people down, and regardless of my role, my building, and my district, I never will. Sparking change will always and forever be a priority.

Leadership Treasure Hunt
(Find This)

Where is "one and done" learning happening
in your building? What can you do about it?

Navigating the Seas
(Think about This)

How can you play a role in continuing learning experiences
that were truly impactful for teachers, for students, and even
for administrators? Think about what struck you as powerful
that you were sad to see disappear. Fight to get it back.

Charting the Course
(Take Action)

Make a commitment right now to tap into your creativity. Make a commitment right now to do something that
will transform "one and done" learning into something
more consistent, something more powerful, something
with greater impact. Whether it is with your students,
colleagues, or administrators, work relentlessly to infuse
it into your classroom or building culture.

Share your thoughts and ideas!
#LeadLAP

It is Time to Passion UP

You have to consider how your words and actions
will impact others, but if you play it too safe,
you'll never accomplish anything truly great.

–Shelley Burgess and Beth Houf, *Lead Like a PIRATE*

If you are interested in something, no matter what
it is, go at it full speed ahead, embrace it with both
arms, hug it, love it, and above all, become passionate
about it. Lukewarm is no good. Hot is no good either.
White hot and passionate is the only thing to be.

–Roald Dahl

learned from the SuperPIRATES of Crew 202 that passion matters, that it should be spread like crazy, and that we all benefit when everyone brings it. I truthfully had a blast my last year in the classroom. It was thrilling. It was a ride. My students and I were "white-hot passionate" about our experiences together and the impact they had.

Over the past few years, I have been asked to remember that not everyone has my enthusiasm. I have been asked to think about how many items I am passionate about, and recently I was asked to consider lessening the load. When I first started in my role, I learned to open up my heart to the passions of others. It made me even more enthusiastic to show up every single day. Our excitement soon fed off of each other, so the thought of simmering my passion and enthusiasm down did not quite sit right. Instead of letting it bother me, I found myself wondering, *What if more educators chose to passion up? What would classrooms, schools, districts, and communities look like?*

I challenge you to think about what *you* are doing to share your passion and enthusiasm so that others will *passion up* with you. A culture I never imagined I would play a role in creating is evolving every day. Had I limited my own passions, I am not sure what school would look like, but fortunately, I do not have to wonder. Had I seen my role in making a difference as linear, I would have missed opportunities to creatively carve paths that did not yet exist. Sometimes I admit it feels like we are stuck in traffic. I have learned, however, that rolling down the windows, blasting some music, and getting people to dance is worth the drive. Eventually, we move forward.

We all know that there are bumps in the road, and it is these bumps that are often the toughest part of our journey. Sometimes we do not see them coming. When you encounter moments that shake you, that get you down, reach out to your crew near and far. Jay Billy, amazing principal and author of *Lead with Culture,* recently shared

> **When you encounter moments that shake you, that get you down, reach out to your crew near and far.**

the quote below by Tony A. Gaskins, Jr., on Twitter. Although hard to digest, it is a quote we must consider.

"The closer you get to excellence in your life, the more friends you'll lose. People love you when you are average because it makes them comfortable. But when you pursue greatness, it makes people uncomfortable. Be prepared to lose some people on your journey."

Yes, we may lose people along the way, but I would like to add to take care of those we do not. Nurture their loyalty and watch what happens. You might even be shocked to see that those you thought you may have lost begin to *notice the impact*. Never forget that we as passionate educators, who believe wholeheartedly in having fun and show up every day to encourage learning that matters, are never ever alone. So please, regardless of your role, keep doing what you are doing and remember to always and relentlessly *passion up*.

Here are a few practices I have recently tried that have helped me influence a culture where *passion up* is becoming more popular every single day.

Break Your Title

Naturally my role focuses on technology to enhance learning, but over the past year, I taught myself how to play the ukulele, cardio drummed with colleagues, ran relay races at Field Day, and led a dance with students, teachers, and administrators in front of the whole school. I even dared to join our Culture Club's "Throwback

Thursday" leaving my *Teach Like a PIRATE* shirt as the only recognizable piece of my attire. (Special thanks to our fabulous art teacher and crewmate, Bonnie Gaus, who seemed to know the perfect look for me.) When we give ourselves permission to be who we are, it inspires others around us to do the same. This sense of freedom is hard to ignore, and even though it may take some longer than others, the likelihood of resisting fun decreases when the joy we breathe in is unavoidable.

Believe in Your Colleagues

Tell your colleagues they rock as often as absolutely possible. This starts by walking with our heads held high enough to make eye contact. Too often we are so incredibly preoccupied that we stop using our senses. This is dangerous because, as humans (even when we do not show it!), we want to be noticed. Aaron Hogan in *Shattering the Perfect Teacher Myth* discusses the idea that students need to be loved, valued, and known. I think the same is true for educators and not just for staff but also administrators. The golden secret I have come to learn is that what matters most is not so much who notices you but the fact that someone did.

In *Lead Like a PIRATE*, Shelley Burgess and Beth Houf challenge the reader to "Notice the Impact." As a technology integration specialist, I tweaked the process and made a commitment to write a note to every classroom teacher letting them know their decisions around twenty-first-century learning were indeed making a difference. I thought, at first, it would not matter as much not coming from an administrator. Not only did it matter, but I believe the level of risk-taking I now see happening throughout our building has everything to do with knowing that, without a doubt, we believe in each other.

IMPACT

<u>I</u>ntentional

<u>M</u>akes a difference

<u>P</u>urposeful

<u>A</u>ctive

<u>C</u>reative

<u>T</u>imely

Dear _____,

I noticed that

Give Your Administrators Some Love. They Often Need It the Most!

In *Kids Deserve It*, Todd Nesloney and Adam Welcome brilliantly put together a list compiled from kids, parents, teachers, and administrators based on the following question: *"What do you wish more people knew about your role?"* I am not sure why. Maybe it is because some of my closest friends in the world are administrators, but I was drawn to that particular page. And the statement that truly resonated with me was this one: "I wish you knew how lonely the administrator job can feel at times."

One day as I was "Twitter coaching" my principal, I noticed her writing short notes of appreciation to teachers as she left their classrooms. I immediately wondered who was writing a note for her. I did not try to find the answer. I simply took a piece of paper and a pen and got busy. Not only did I receive an email later that day, but she actually tweeted her excitement with an image of people jumping. The caption read, "What it feels like to be recognized by a colleague." We can never underestimate the human need to be noticed, regardless of our roles.

Lead Up

Whether it is your direct administrators, your superintendent, school committee, or even the mayor, leading up is always a possibility. In my experience, it is the best administrators who listen to the voices of teachers and act on what they hear. Teachers have the most direct contact with students, and it is the students we show up for every single day. The success of a district relies on its teachers. Knowing this, we must believe that we have the power to make a difference and to lead up. When I met with my superintendent about the book study, I also shared ideas about professional development, including that teachers were hungry for more choice, voice, and relevancy. She asked to borrow *Learner Centered Innovation*, took *Lead Like a PIRATE* happily, and most importantly, she listened. If we all believe that anyone can lead, we must also believe that anyone can be led. Make this a reality for you and your district.

Break the Script

"Target a specific moment and then challenge yourself: How can I elevate it? Spark insight? Boost the sense of connection? Life is full of 'form letter in an envelope' moments, waiting to be transformed into something special." I love that quote from Chip Heath and Dan Heath in *The Power of Moments*. As educators, we live in a world of planning. Lesson plans, common planning time, plan books, plan A, B, and even C. It almost goes against a teacher's instinct to "break the script." But what if breaking the script was part of the plan? What if it was driven with intention to spark extraordinary experiences for students, staff, and administrators? What if we were the spark? Check out a video (Yes, I am super passionate about creating and sharing videos!) that captures breaking the script with a lesson that sparked one memorable moment that became many. (bit.ly/Breakthescript)

Summary

The potential for leading with passion is too sacred not to tap into. When we find comfort in status quo and rely on compliance to lead the way, real change increases its distance. Whether you are like me, born with "too much energy," or rely on calmness to help you lead, or somewhere in the middle, find your path to *passion up*. Make sure you inspire those around you to do the same.

Leadership Treasure Hunt (Find This)

Where does passion exist in your building? Who is leading with passion? Who is following? What can you learn from your colleagues who are bringing passion to work every day?

 ## Navigating the Seas (Think about This)

Are you leading with passion? If not, what is holding you back? A teacher once told me that there was no time for her to teach with passion, and she was truly sad. How can we change this mindset for teachers? For administrators?

 ## Charting the Course (Take Action)

Whether you are the one choosing to *passion up* and inspire those around you or you are following the lead of someone who is already doing it, choose a way that you can embrace what matters most to you. Bring it to school every single day. Just as much as we need leaders (and maybe even more!) we need people who are willing to follow the "lone nut" who is daring to try something new or different. (If you're curious about what it means to be a "lone nut," check out Derek Sivers' video for inspiration and a laugh: bit.ly/Lonenut.) Passion is contagious. Regardless of where you grab it from, there is no such thing as taking too much.

Share your thoughts and ideas!
#LeadLAP

The Journey of a PIRATE Superintendent Who Was Inspired by Her PIRATE Principal

Crystal M. Edwards, EdD, superintendent,
Lynchburg City Schools, Virginia

I am not sure when it actually occurred. Perhaps it began when I first read *Teach Like a PIRATE*. Or maybe it was the day I was lurking on Twitter learning about #tlap. Some say it was after of one my principals dressed up as a pirate during a faculty meeting. It could have been that day that Dave Burgess visited our school district. Regardless of the exact time, I became a PIRATE . . . and there was no going back!

My transformation was not easy at first. While *Teach Like a PIRATE* was loaded with great tips, inspirational ideas, and ready-to-use classroom strategies, my reality was that I had no classroom to transform into an experiential learning environment for kids. I did not spend my nights planning engaging lessons that reflected my students' interests. I had no bulletin boards to post mystery messages that would challenge young minds. My day did not start with me cooking for, singing to, or dancing with my students as we explored other cultures. Nope, I was not a teacher . . . I was a superintendent. Then it dawned on me that I needed to think outside of the box. In fact, I needed to get out of the box altogether.

I found myself taking Shelley and Beth's ANCHOR challenge to a new level. (ANCHOR stands for Appreciation, Notice the Impact, Collaborative Conversation, Honor Voice and Choice, Offer Support, and Reflect.) I sent my principals, supervisors, and assistant principals appreciation notes. I began to notice the wonderful things administrators did to enhance the learning environment for their staff and students. I praised my administrators who joined PLNs and participated in professional learning with colleagues in other districts. Our traditional principal observation/evaluation protocols were transformed into collaborative conversations. And most importantly, reflection was at the heart of these collaborative conversations. Our entire organizational structure was changing. We even modified our district logo to convey our commitment to PIRATE teaching.

During the summer break, I received a copy of *Lead Like a PIRATE*, and it all fell into place. In August, I found myself sending thank-you notes to my administrators' families, highlighting why my administrators were so amazing. *Lead Like a PIRATE* taught me the value of sharing our stories, so during our new-staff orientation, I dressed up as Queen Nandi and engaged my staff in a conversation about equity, resilience, and perseverance, my #SuperYouFun power. It was not your ordinary new staff orientation!

I was fortunate to be selected to teach an advanced supervision and evaluation class for aspiring administrators. My first lesson—"Get the Right People on the Ship." Throughout my three-day class, I shared my passions, developed a rapport with my aspiring administrators, taught them to ask challenging questions, and ramped up the enthusiasm with various TLAP hooks. At the end of my session, I was proud to commission a new set of "captains" who understood that supervision begins with the interview and set the expectation for good teaching. It was rewarding to see these passionate aspiring administrators knocking the doors down to get into our schools to make a difference.

SAILING BEYOND
YOUR OWN TITLE

Model what you hope for in your teachers
and your students. Take risks, try new things,
and don't be afraid to have fun doing it.

–Shelley Burgess and Beth Houf, *Lead Like a PIRATE*

No matter what your position, you can create change.
If you are struggling to do so, maybe you are trying to
pick up all the snow at once. Just grab a handful, pack
it tight, and then start pushing. Change is a lot easier
when you're rolling snowballs downhill.

–Dave Burgess

I may not control when I work with our staff, but I LEAD with every part of my being during every minute I get.

I may not control when I work with each class, but I LEAD by filling every second of teaching with empowerment (and some humor!).

I may not make the BIG decisions, but I LEAD by reaching out to administrators, proving to them I can make a difference with my heart and mind.

I may not create the master schedule, but I LEAD by creating my own in hopes that I inspire twenty-first-century learning in every classroom.

I may not control our school Twitter account, but I LEAD by convincing teachers to take the awesome things they are doing and share them with the world.

I may not have written our mission statement, but I LEAD by putting students and teachers on a mission to discover what makes them unique.

I am in a non-administrative role, but I chose to be a leader. Your final challenge is to make your role come to life like never before. Write your own journey and make sure you share it because the world needs your brand of awesome and nothing less.

Remember to . . .

Believe you have the power to lead beyond what has been defined for you every single day by being yourself and who you choose to become.

Never become a victim of title suffocation. We all ache to be understood, so give people every opportunity in the world to understand you—all of you.

Work relentlessly to master resilience when faced with doubt—because there will be doubt, but you've got this.

Continue to tell yourself that most educators, even if buried under those full plates, crave to be inspired, so work tirelessly to build your crew near and far.

On your hardest days, remember that, as Dave Burgess says, we are in this "life-changing business" together, we are never alone, and we must always remember that it is the PIRATE in all of us that keeps us going.

If we stay true to our PIRATE roots, we can find opportunities to lead in every kind of culture. When it's thriving, we must nurture it every single day. We must fight for it as well as for the leaders who bring their awesome to school, to our district, and to our community. Support them publicly, let it be known who they are, who you are, and share your excitement to be a follower. Not only will you make your culture stronger, but leaders who are able to follow are more impactful because of it.

When a culture is hurting, and we experience moments of pain, we must remind ourselves that it's in these moments that our colleagues, students, and even administrators need us more than ever. Chances are that if you're facing challenges, so are those around you. Do not be afraid to speak up. You may be surprised by the power we each hold, regardless of our titles when we have the courage to do what is right.

As you continue your leadership journey and as I continue mine, here are just a few lines for all of us to hold onto. The most important lesson I learned from the SuperPIRATES of Crew 202 is that those who are willing to dance with you or who inspire you to dance will embrace your unique rhythm as well as your crazy moves. Surround yourself with these people every day, near and far, and never, ever forget to believe in who you are.

BRING NILI BARTLEY TO YOUR SCHOOL OR DISTRICT

With high energy, connection, and often times playing musical instruments, Nili leads unique professional development sessions for educators and school leaders. She has presented at conferences such as ISTE, MassCUE, ASCD's Empower, Tomorrow's Classrooms Today, and Natick's Innovation and Learning Summit. Some of her most popular session topics include . . .

- The Connected Educator
- Leading from any Role
- Lessons Learned from *Lead Like a PIRATE*
- The 21st Century Classroom
- Approaches and Platforms for Strength- and Passion-Based Learning
- Genius Hour
- Putting Edcamp into Action for Teachers and Students
- The SuperYou Fundation
- BrainPOP
- Online Creation and Assessment Tools
- Storytelling through Video

More from
DAVE BURGESS Consulting, Inc.

Since 2012, DBCI has been publishing books that inspire and equip educators to be their best. For more information on our DBCI titles or to purchase bulk orders for your school, district, or book study, visit **DaveBurgessConsulting.com/DBCBooks**.

More from the Like a PIRATE Series

Teach Like a PIRATE by Dave Burgess

Explore Like a Pirate by Michael Matera

Learn Like a Pirate by Paul Solarz

Play Like a Pirate by Quinn Rollins

Run Like a Pirate by Adam Welcome

Lead Like a PIRATE Series

Lead Like a PIRATE by Shelley Burgess and Beth Houf

Balance Like a Pirate by Jessica Cabeen, Jessica Johnson, and Sarah Johnson

Lead with Culture by Jay Billy

Lead with Literacy by Mandy Ellis

Leadership & School Culture

Culturize by Jimmy Casas

Escaping the School Leader's Dunk Tank by Rebecca Coda and Rick Jetter

The Innovator's Mindset by George Couros

Kids Deserve It! by Todd Nesloney and Adam Welcome

Let Them Speak by Rebecca Coda and Rick

Start. Right. Now. by Todd Whitaker, Jeffrey Zoul, and
  Jimmy Casas

Stop. Right. Now. by Jimmy Casas and Jeffrey Zoul Jetter

The Limitless School by Abe Hege and Adam Dovico

The Pepper Effect by Sean Gaillard

The Principled Principal by Jeffrey Zoul and
  Anthony McConnell

The Secret Solution by Todd Whitaker, Sam Miller, and
  Ryan Donlan

They Call Me "Mr. De" by Frank DeAngelis

Unmapped Potential by Julie Hasson and Missy Lennard

Your School Rocks by Ryan McLane and Eric Lowe

Technology & Tools

50 Things You Can Do with Google Classroom by Alice Keeler
  and Libbi Miller

50 Things to Go Further with Google Classroom by Alice
Keeler
  and Libbi Miller

140 Twitter Tips for Educators by Brad Currie, Billy Krakower,
  and Scott Rocco

Code Breaker by Brian Aspinall

Creatively Productive by Lisa Johnson

Google Apps for Littles by Christine Pinto and Alice Keeler

Master the Media by Julie Smith

Shake Up Learning by Kasey Bell

Social LEADia by Jennifer Casa-Todd

Teaching Math with Google Apps by Alice Keeler and
Diana Herrington

Teaching Methods & Materials

All 4s and 5s by Andrew Sharos
Ditch That Homework by Matt Miller and Alice Keeler
Ditch That Textbook by Matt Miller
Educated by Design by Michael Cohen
The EduProtocol Field Guide by Marlena Hebern and
Jon Corippo
Instant Relevance by Denis Sheeran
LAUNCH by John Spencer and A.J. Juliani
Make Learning MAGICAL by Tisha Richmond
Pure Genius by Don Wettrick
Shift This! by Joy Kirr
Spark Learning by Ramsey Musallam
Sparks in the Dark by Travis Crowder and Todd Nesloney
Table Talk Math by John Stevens
The Classroom Chef by John Stevens and Matt Vaudrey
The Wild Card by Hope and Wade King
The Writing on the Classroom Wall by Steve Wyborney

Inspiration, Professional Growth, & Personal Development

The Four O'Clock Faculty by Rich Czyz
Be REAL by Tara Martin
Be the One for Kids by Ryan Sheehy
The EduNinja Mindset by Jennifer Burdis
How Much Water Do We Have? by Pete and Kris Nunweiler
P Is for Pirate by Dave and Shelley Burgess
The Path to Serendipity by Allyson Aspey

Sanctuaries by Dan Tricarico

Shattering the Perfect Teacher Myth by Aaron Hogan

Stories from Webb by Todd Nesloney

Talk to Me by Kim Bearden

The Zen Teacher by Dan Tricarico

Children's Books

Dolphins in Trees by Aaron Polansky

The Princes of Serendip by Allyson Apsey

About the Author

Nili Bartley is currently a technology teacher and integration specialist at Wilson Middle School in Natick, Massachusetts. Nili is passionate about bringing unconventional learning to students and colleagues and empowering them to bring their strengths and passions to school every single day. After an eleven year adventure in the classroom inspiring students to lead, Nili's technology integration role at the elementary level for the next three years pushed her to see the importance of a thriving culture. Through coaching colleagues and implementing innovative ideas, Nili was able to serve as a catalyst, sparking positive change in her buildings as well as her school district. Now in a new role and district, Nili is bringing her experiences with her and is certainly creating new ones. A MassCUE Committee Member, BrainPOP Certified Educator, enthusiastic presenter, and blog author, Nili is committed to sharing her passions beyond the school community and is always excited to connect with other educators.

Made in the USA
Monee, IL
10 March 2021